On the Reappraisal
of Keynesian Economics

On the Reappraisal of Keynesian Economics

A revised and extended version of a University Special Lecture delivered at Queen Mary College in the University of London on 7th December 1970.

A.G. Hines
Professor of Economics, University of Durham

Martin Robertson & Company Ltd

First published 1971 by
Martin Robertson & Company Ltd
108 Cowley Road, Oxford OX4 1JF

Reprinted 1972 and 1978

ISBN 0 85520 004 9

Set by The Palantype Organisation Ltd
Printed by photolithography and made in Great Britain
at the Pitman Press, Bath

Contents

I The (Neo)-Classical Resurgence

Within the past five years the work of Clower, Leijonhufvud and others[1]* has re-awakened interest in the question of what constitutes the theoretical basis of the 'Keynesian' revolution.

Before this there had been a consensus among the majority and perhaps dominant school in the profession as to the nature of Keynes' contribution to economics. That consensus was not very flattering to Keynes' claim to have produced a general theory which provided a synthesis between the theory of value and the theory of money. For the consensus asserted that Keynes had really taken the then current model, and had arbitrarily imposed certain restrictions upon it — converting certain functions into constants, setting certain price elasticities equal to infinity or to zero — and then had claimed not only to have refuted the Classical model but also to have provided a more general theory. As was pointed out during the great debate, to make that kind of claim and to make it stick, one has to take on a theory on its own grounds. According to the consensus, this is precisely what Keynes had failed to do. It would not be overstating the position to say that the prevailing view was that so far as pure theory was concerned Keynes would have been well advised not to have written the General Theory at all (19)*. He should have written a note in the Economic Journal (or perhaps more appropriately written a letter to 'The Times') making the rather obvious observation that in modern capitalist economies money wages are rigid in a downward direction. It would also have helped if he had not clouded the issue by making incantatory noises about the "dark forces, of time and ignorance which envelop our times", and by introducing funny mechanical toys such as the multiplier.

---

* These superior figures refer to notes at the end of each chapter. Figures in brackets refer to the Bibliography at the end of the book.

If proof were required that this was in fact the dominant view of the Keynesian revolution one has only to look at the Neo-Classical resurgence, the revival of the Quantity Theory or the work of Patinkin and the character of the debate which surrounded it[2]. True, there still existed in various corners of England some followers of Keynes. But then the English are well known for their love and reverence for ancient monuments and relics.

The standard models in terms of which the debate was conducted are well known and it is not necessary to write them down[3]. The usual argument is familiar. Given wage and price flexibility, the equations of the labour market determine a market-clearing real wage rate at full employment of labour. Since the historically given capital stock is thrown on to the market in perfectly inelastic supply, the production function determines the maximum obtainable level of output. Given output, the equilibrium condition in the market for commodities simultaneously determines the rate of interest and the proportion of its income which the community wishes to consume currently, and the proportion which it wishes to use to add to the man-made means of production. With real income and the rate of interest determined, the equilibrium condition in the money market determines the price level for a given stock of money. This result is not vitiated by adding to the model an asset demand for money and by setting its partial derivative with respect to the rate of interest equal to infinity. Nor is it affected by setting the elasticities of the expenditure sector with respect to the rate of interest close to, or equal to, zero. So long as there is a stock of outside government debt, which is assumed to be the net worth of the private sector, under a regime of wage and price flexibility the solution state of the model exhibits full employment, i.e. it lies on the physical transformation frontier of society.

Naturally, if one assumes that one price, the money price of labour, is rigid because workers are organised in trade unions and/or suffer from money illusion, then it follows trivially that for a given stock of money the model no longer necessarily yields a unique full-employment solution. In this context the introduction of a speculative demand for money together with the money illusion which is allegedly built into it does not matter. It simply weakens the strong version of the quantity theory of money.

It had to be admitted that the logical validity of the Classical model depended ultimately on the existence of a stock of outside money and the indifference of the public sector to the size of its liabilities. It was agreed that this was a slender reed on which to lean in a situation in which the real wage rate was too high. Consideration of time lags, the relevant magnitudes of the response of aggregate expenditure to changes in net worth, possible perverse expectations and so on indicated that both social justice and efficiency in the choice of instruments required the use of fiscal and monetary policies to correct any chance departure from the equilibrium state. As Leijonhufvud points out, it was this admission which was responsible for the recent truce and the burial of the Keynes vs. Classics debate. For the theorists were prepared to concede to those with a more practical turn of mind that the so called 'Keynes special case' is the one which is empirically relevant for short run policy. The classics won the intellectual battle; Keynes won the policy war. Again the victorious theorists were too polite to point out that 'Keynesian' policies were being advocated by a varied assortment of men long before the General Theory appeared.

This state of affairs has been rudely shattered by the work of Clower and Leijonhufvud. For, if they are correct — as indeed they are correct — Keynes' claim is substantiated or, at the very least, is still on the agenda. A major revision and abandonment of certain well entrenched views is in order, and the theoretical questions which Keynes posed still stand at the frontier of on-going research in our subject. For their thesis is that Keynes' under-employment state (it is a matter of semantics whether we call it an equilibrium state, since equilibrium is nothing more than a short-hand term for the set of values of the variables that satisfies the equations of a given model) can be shown to exist independently of liquidity traps, the equality of savings and investment requiring a non-feasible negative price vector, money illusion, rigid wages, etc.

Let me summarise, or rather give my own interpretation of the core of their contention.

NOTES

1 Clower's seminal paper is (5). Its logical growth is (6) and other papers. Leijonhufvud's monumentally scholarly work (22) builds upon and extends Clower's ideas and contains original analysis of such matters as the theory of liquidity preference and

the Keynes' wealth effect. Davidson's paper (8) respecifies the demand function for money in a manner which is appropriate to dynamic analysis. Building on the foregoing studies, Hines (14) has presented a reappraisal of the Keynesian theory of short run movements in the rate of interest.

2   The Neo-Classical resurgence manifests itself in almost all branches of economics. Two relevant examples are (i) the dominance of growth models which are concerned with the existence, stability and comparative dynamics of steady states in which it is assumed that full employment is automatically maintained at all points in time and (ii) the re-emergence of theories in which all unemployment is voluntary and frictional at an invariant full employment level of activity. The revival of the Quantity Theory and the associated monetarist counter-revolution is well documented in Friedman (9). Patinkin's classic book (27) is an elegant re-statement of the full employment statics of the Walrasian general equilibrium system.

3   Examples of the standard model are to be found in Modigiliani (24, 25), Patinkin (27), Bailey (3).

II The Reappraisal of Keynes' Theory of Employment

Keynes was well aware that if he was to show that he had a theory which was more general than that of his predecessors, he had to take on their theory on its own grounds. Consequently, he accepted the following (Neo)-Classical assumptions.

(a) Households are rational in the sense that they maximise well-ordered utility functions irrespective of whether the arguments of these functions are contemporaneously available commodities or present and future commodities.

(b) Firms maximise profits.

(c) Well-behaved physical transformation functions exist.

(d) There is a 'large' number of traders on each side of each market.

(e) Price incentives are effective.

(f) Transactors do not suffer from money illusion.

His challenge went to the very heart of Neo-Classical theory, for, as Leijonhufvud points out: "in a large system where decision making is decentralised, the efficient working of the price mechanism requires that it fulfils two functions simultaneously (a) prices should <u>disseminate the information</u> necessary to co-ordinate the economic activities and plans of the independent transactors and (b) prices should <u>provide the incentives</u> for transactors to adjust their activities in such manner that they become consistent in the aggregate." (22). In other words if the market clearing vector of relative prices (which is assumed to exist) is known by all transactors, and if each transactor adjusts to these parameters, the system simultaneously generates an optimal allocation of resources and ensures that they are fully employed. To demonstrate his thesis Keynes was willing to accept the proposition that price incentives are effective. What he denied was that the price system disseminates the appropriate information with sufficient efficiency to guarantee the full employment of the economy's resources, at any rate in the short-run.

The question of the dissemination of information concerning the market clearing price vector has worried the truly great minds of our profession. Adam Smith thought that it was all done by 'the invisible hand'; Edgeworth allowed his traders to 're-contract'; Walras had an auctioneer who, without cost to the system, called out the prices. Walras made the proviso, which is very apposite in this context, that contracts were not binding and no trade was to take place until the market clearing vector of prices was finally announced. Moreover, if the system was subjected to some exogenous disturbance, say a change in tastes or in technology, the auctioneer would immediately announce the new market clearing price vector and, given the implied infinite velocity of price adjustments, the system would immediately adjust to its new optimal position. If we extend the argument to an economy in which accumulation is taking place and in which expenditure plans extend over n time periods, the optimal operation of such an economy requires that the Walrasian auctioneer should disseminate the information concerning the vector of inter-temporal relative prices which would simultaneously clear all present and future markets.

But what is the situation if, as Keynes insisted, there is no such auctioneer? We immediately face a dilemma. For, as Arrow (2) points out, if each transactor is a price taker, who is left over to make the price? Let us imagine that the going price vector is somehow correct; then everything is satisfactory. But now let the system be subject to some exogenous disturbance such that it requires a new market clearing vector if plans are to mesh in the aggregate. What then? It is clear that we are no longer in a state of perfect competition. Perfect competition requires that each transactor be able to buy and sell as much as he wishes at going prices and this clearly cannot happen at a wrong set of relative prices. As long as disequilibrium exists each optimising transactor must behave like a monopolist since he faces downward sloping demand and upward sloping supply curves along which he must search for the correct combination of prices and/or quantities. And we are immediately faced with the probability that trade may take place at false prices.

In an attempt to be more realistic than Walras and Edgeworth, Hicks (11) wished to generalise his analysis of the determination of relative prices to markets in which there is no auctioneer and/or in which re-contracting is not permitted. He therefore had to admit the possibility of false trading at disequilibrium prices. However, he wished to show that the same equilibrium price set is attainable as in the case in which all trade takes place at equilibrium prices. Consequently, he assumed that the only effect of false trading would be a re-distribution of income between buyers and sellers and that the income effects of such re-distribution would be small, because the volume of false trading would be small and would occur at prices which did not deviate much from the set of equilibrium prices and would in any case tend to cancel out on both sides of the market "if any intelligence is shown in price fixing". Hicks observed "that a certain degree of indeterminateness is nearly always imparted by income effects to the laws of economic theory" and that false trading intensifies this indeterminateness. However, he did not really offer a solution to the question of how the system behaves when there is false trading. For this theoretical issue cannot be settled by the introduction of an empirical assumption which amounts to saying no more than "that income effects can be ignored if they are sufficiently unimportant to be neglected."(5)

What then are we to assume about the behaviour of the typical transactor who holds stocks of assets such as labour, money, bonds, capital goods, etc., and who must in a disequilibrium situation make some assumption about expected market prices and/or quantities? The assumption made by Keynes' predecessors and by the majority of post-Keynesians is that the elasticity of price expectations is unity. Each transactor regards the first set of prices that emerge in the wake of a disturbance as correct. If each transactor acts immediately upon this belief then unemployed resources cannot emerge even though the resulting situation may not be Pareto optimal. But is this the most reasonable assumption to make? Why, as this argument implies, should transactors regard the present value of their assets as being perfectly variable? Why is it rational for transactors who have some memory and who make plans for the future to passively regard such changes in their net worth as normal?

Imagine a worker who, because of some change which results in a reduction in the demand for his labour, is made unemployed or can only keep his present job by accepting a substantial cut in his money wages. He must decide whether to accept this cut or choose to become unemployed. To make a decision, he has to form a view as to whether the new situation is local or is generalised, is permanent or is temporary. If he regards the situation as localised and temporary, so that the previous wage rate will presently be restored, then this implies that he regards that previous wage as normal. He will therefore choose to become unemployed (or more likely to be laid off by his employers without being offered the alternative of accepting a lower wage). He must then begin a search for employment at the expected wage, balancing the cost of search against the probability of obtaining a better offer. At each stage he must compare the present value of the income streams which will emerge if he accepts the next offer against that which he would obtain at his expected best offer, the expected wage itself being a decreasing function of the length of search. Several writers have shown that the inescapable consequence of such phenomena is the emergence of unemployed resources which can be regarded at the micro level as a reservation demand on the part of the owner for the services of his own assets.

Or again, consider the position of a bond holder. The typical ultimate asset holder in Keynes' theory is an individual in the middle of his life cycle who owns a share in the system's physical capital. Given the assumption that more roundabout processes are physically more productive than less roundabout ones — a Cassellian proposition which begs the index number question — the economy is tempted by the profitability of 'long' processes to carry a stock of illiquid assets. But this stock will turn over more slowly than households want. Our typical asset holder from some future date onwards plans to consume in excess of current gross incomes, the amounts and dates of the necessary encashments being presently uncertain. But the maturity structure of his representative share in the system's capital stock is assumed to be too long to match this encashment schedule. He is subject to capital uncertainty since assets may have to be sold at a loss to meet planned encashments. The representative transactor who is presumed to be a risk averter must be offered some compensation for the risk which this speculative position entails, just as a bank must be offered a yield differential between deposits and earning assets in order to borrow short and lend long. Now suppose that there is a fall in bond prices. The bond holder (who like the worker is assumed to have inelastic price expectations) will, as a risk averting optimiser, buy bonds on the expectation of a capital gain if he regards the previous price as normal, i.e. he will re-arrange his portfolio so that on balance it moves towards the less liquid end of the maturity spectrum. (The argument is symmetrical for a fall in the interest rate.) This is, of course, the basis of the doctrine of liquidity preference.

Exactly the same analysis holds for the owner of any other asset, including entrepreneurs who invest directly in capital goods. Thus in Keynes' short-run model every transactor is assumed to have inelastic price expectations; it is not an assumption which applies exclusively to the holders of bonds.

We are therefore in a world whose differences from its classical predecessors flow from the failure of the price mechanism to disseminate the information which is required to co-ordinate the plans of transactors both now and in the future. It is a world of inelastic expectations, reservation demands and adjustment costs. Instead of a known vector of relative prices of currently produced commodities, prices are the outcome of a non-tâtonnement search procedure. Moreover, whereas one can conceive of changes in institutional arrangements which would improve the dissemination of information concerning the market clearing vector of current relative prices, in principle the provision of adequate information concerning the appropriate inter-temporal price vector of an uncertain future appears to be impossible. Instead of a known vector of inter-temporal prices we therefore have two phenomena: (a) the long term state of expectations, alias the marginal efficiency of capital which summarises entrepreneurial conjectures about the prospective income streams to be obtained from outlays on physical capital; (b) liquidity preference which determines the composition of portfolios with respect to the continuum of assets with varying dates to maturity. Hence, if plans are to be consistent in the aggregate in the absence of the appropriate forward markets, both the marginal efficiency of capital and the structure of asset prices — 'the rate of interest' — must correctly anticipate and reflect future prices and quantities in commodity and financial markets.

Now there is a forward market of sorts in the economy. It is the stock exchange. But this market does not transmit the information that would be provided by the Walrasian auctioneer. For, as Keynes pointed out, although there is the activity of 'enterprise' in this market – the genuine attempt, on imperfect information, to forecast the future yields from sources of income and to act upon such forecasts – there is also the activity of 'speculation'. And in times of disequilibrium the latter easily dominate the former. But it is just at such times that the activity of enterprise should dominate if the effects of the workings of this market are to be stabilising rather than de-stabilising.

Keynes' problem then was to analyse "the economic behaviour of the present under the influence of changing ideas about the future", noting that "it is by reason of the existence of durable equipment that the future is linked to the present". What triggers off a cumulative contraction in the General Theory is a failure in the co-ordination of production, trading and consumption plans in the future. The exogenous disturbances with which Keynes was concerned were either a change in the long run state of expectations or a change in tastes which altered the propensity to save or the form in which wealth holders chose to hold their assets.

We must now investigate the system-wide implications with respect to the level of aggregate output and employment of any such disturbance.

In a barter system where all commodities are directly tradeable against each other the system-wide consequences of such disturbances are not clear. But the Keynesian system is a monetary economy, i.e. it is a system in which money is the only commodity which is directly tradeable in all markets[4]. Here the system-wide implictions are abundantly clear.

In a money economy it is necessary to distinguish between desire (which may be based on feasible transformation possibilities) and effective demand – desires backed by the ability to pay in cash. In such an economy it is money offers to buy and to sell which take over the role of the system of relative prices and act as the mechanism which transmits the relevant market signals to transactors. But this means, as Clower has pointed out, that we must now distinguish between notional excess demands – excess demands which reflect the underlying real transformation possibilities of the system – and actual or effective excess demands – those which are backed by the ability to pay in money and which therefore constitute relevant market signals. These two sets of excess demands are only equal when the system is in a full equilibrium. What this means is that except in a full equilibrium in which each excess demand is zero, Walras' Law does not hold as between notional and effective excess demands[5].

Walras' Law is the proposition that the sum of the value of all excess demands is zero, i.e.

$$\sum_{i=1}^{n} P_i q_i = 0, \ q_i \equiv D_i - S_i.$$

In a barter economy with a tâtonnement mechanism such that trade never takes place at 'false' prices, all excess demand functions hold simultaneously and "the offer of any commodity is an exercise of effective purchasing power over any other commodity" (6). Hence Walras' Law follows by logical necessity. This is not the case in a money economy since every act of exchange between two non-monetary commodities is necessarily indirect. All this does not matter in full equilibrium when all excess demands are zero. Then Walras' Law does hold. However, in a state of transactor disequilibrium, Walras' Law as usually defined does not hold. Thus consider an equilibrium which is disturbed by the decision of some transactor to increase his consumption (or holdings) or some commodity i by supplying some other commodity j to the market. In a barter economy with all other excess demand functions equal to zero, we would simply write $X_i = -X_j$ where X_i and X_j are the value of the excess demand for the ith and jth good respectively. But in a monetary economy, this procedure is not appropriate unless the jth commodity is money. If it is not money, then in order to make his plans effective the individual must first exchange the jth commodity for money and, if he is successful, he then exchanges money for the ith commodity. And, since in a non-tâtonnement system the actual vector of prices might be such that plans to demand money (plans to supply goods, bonds or factor services) may not be achieved, i.e. actual sales may fall short of or exceed planned sales, the contingent plans to demand goods, bonds and money to hold as an asset stand subject to revision. Clower has analysed what this involves for the optimising transactor as a 'dual decision hypothesis'. Transactors maximise their utility subject to the constraint of their notional income. If their realised and notional incomes are equal, the system is in a full equilibrium and the excess demand functions generated by the solution to the familiar constrained maximisation problem yield relevant market signals. But if actual incomes are not equal to notional incomes a second round of decision making is in order: the transactor must maximise utility subject to the constraint of realised income which is the money value of the receipts from the sale of factor services. It is the resulting income-constrained excess demand functions which provide relevant market signals.

Now suppose that, starting from a position of equilibrium, there is an exogenous change in the state of long term expectations such that entrepreneurs re-evaluate in a downward direction the prospective yields from the services of capital goods and that this results in a reduction in planned investment expenditures at each level of the rate of interest. In the classical full information system, there is a fall in the interest rate which increases the consumption income ratio at an unchanged level of output and employment. In Keynes' theory there is an implication for the level of output and employment. The rate of interest does fall: but its fall is insufficient to equate savings and investment at an unchanged level of income. The limitation in the fall of the interest rate is due to the existence of liquidity preference. Speculators who consider that the rise in bond prices will be reversed, offer savers existing bonds from their portfolios (equal in value to the reduced supply of the investors in capital goods) in exchange for money and hoard the proceeds of sale. In these circumstances, there is a fall in expenditure on new capital goods, and given the assumptions which we have already made, unemployed resources emerge in this sector before any countervailing effects of the possible unwinding of the speculative position taken up by the 'bears' can make itself felt.

Unemployed resources emerge because of the sequence of trades which is assumed to take place in a production economy in which contracts are made in terms of money. In the absence of a market clearing vector of prices which is known, entrepreneurs plan their output on the basis of the level of demand which they expect to rule in the future and which depends in part upon a weighted average of past levels of sales. Given planned output, firms enter into price contracts, fixed for a stated period, for the services of productive resources. Faced with an unexpected fall in demand, entrepreneurs who are assumed to have inelastic price expectations do not reduce the price of their output within the unit period by an amount which is sufficient to dispose of their current output. They are therefore faced with an unintended accumulation of inventories at the end of the period. Even if they plan to make some reduction in the price of output in the next period, they will now reduce the amount of factor services for which they will contract at the end of the current period, especially since the assumption of inelastic price expectations also applies to the owners of these productive services so that they would not accept a reduction in rates of remuneration sufficient to keep their factors employed in the same establishment.

Now consider an unemployed worker in this sector who now begins a search for a wage rate which is consistent with his current estimate of the present value of his labour services. His notional excess supply of labour does not provide him with the means to transmit relevant information concerning his corresponding excess demand for goods. How is he to maintain his desired levels of expenditure? He could run down any accumulated non-labour assets. But then he must do this in a situation in which uncertainty about their realisable value has increased. He could try to borrow, offering as collateral his human and/or non-human wealth. But, in addition to his uncertain but inelastic expectations about their present values, lending institutions themselves have no hard knowledge but must conjecture about the value of the collateral which is being offered. Moreover, in the postulated situation, lending institutions are also attempting to increase the liquidity of their portfolios. The costs of being unemployed are high and we may expect downward revisions in the worker's reservation price as the unemployment state persists. But so long as the elasticity of expectations is less than unity in Keynes' short period, the worker in the sector in which the disturbance first occurs, will have an actual income which is less than his notional income and, since actual income now constitutes a binding constraint on actual behaviour, effective demands are now reduced in markets in which the initial shock may have had no impact. Unemployed resources now emerge in these markets and "the search instituted by unemployed workers and producers with excess capacity will yield information on 'effective' demands not on 'notional' demands. The 'multiplier' repercussions thus set in motion make the information acquired 'dated' even while it is being gathered"(22). To each set of trades which takes place there corresponds a set of wrong relative prices which are themselves unkown to all transactors. There is no reason to assume (at any rate without further specification) that in the short-run the system is converging to the correct vector of relative prices. Rather, as Keynes' theory implies, the observed price and quantity changes are deviation amplifying and the system probably contracts to a floor which is set by the given stock of money.

The same analysis holds if there is an increase in the propensity to save which is the result of a change in tastes such that households wish to alter the time profile of their consumption stream in favour of future consumption. In the classical system, the rate of interest now falls so that the increased demand for bonds which is assumed to be the analogue of the increase in savings is met by new issues by investors. Savings and investment are equated at a higher investment to income ratio and full-employment is maintained. In Keynes' theory, the level of output and employment falls. An act of saving is a plan to increase the transactor's future command over purchasing power in general. Unlike money expenditure on currently produced goods and services, it does not transmit relevant information to producers concerning the specific goods and the combination thereof which will be demanded in the future. In the absence of this information, the relevant inter-temporal price vector is unknown. Consequently, entrepreneurs do not have the same incentive as in the Classical system to shift the composition of their portfolios towards the less liquid end of the maturity spectrum. The rate of interest does fall, but because of liquidity preference its fall is partially stabilised. Just as in the case of the fall in the marginal efficiency of capital, 'bear' speculators offer those who wish to increase their current savings existing bonds from their portfolios and hoard the proceeds of sale. Thus only a fraction of the increased demand for bonds is met by new issues. In these circumstances there is a fall in expenditure on consumer goods which is not offset by the increased expenditure on investment goods. Unemployed resources emerge; the process which we have already described is under way, and when the equality of savings and investment does come about, it is the result of a cumulative contraction in incomes and employment.

Thus, contrary to what has become standard doctrine, liquidity preference – or rather the hypothesis of inelastic price expectations which underlies the notion of liquidity preference – can explain under-employment equilibrium. The multiplier does amplify initial disturbances. For we have been analysing the consequences of false trading in a situation in which the actual vector of relative prices is not only wrong but is unknown. To generate Keynes' under-employment state we simply relinquish the strong, but in the context inappropriate, Classical assumption of infinite velocity of prices and zero velocity of quantities within the unit period. A reversal of the ranking of price and quantity velocities is sufficient. Specifically, the assumption of an absolute rigidity in the money wage rate is not necessary to explain under-employment. Indeed the Keynesian analysis leads to the distinctly non-Classical conclusion that in a general equilibrium model unemployed resources may emerge in the ith market at a correct money price in that market because the money price is wrong in the jth market. In this case, the ith market is the labour market: the jth market is the market for 'bonds'. Moreover, contrary to Walras' Law, the system can attain a (temporary) equilibrium with an excess supply of labour which is not matched by an equivalent value of <u>effective</u> excess demand for goods. The unemployed workers may be said to have an excess demand for money. However, it is notional rather than effective inasmuch as it cannot work "directly on the price system to offset prevailing elements of excess supply"(5). The contingent excess demand for goods is also notional since it cannot be communicated to producers unless and until labour is successfully exchanged for money.

In such a situation, a policy of cutting money wages is a faulty prescription based on a wrong diagnosis. For in Keynes' analysis of advanced capitalist economies, a disequilibrium is usually assumed to originate in a change in long run expectations or in liquidity preference, which generates a rate of interest too high for a general equilibrium. A sufficient cut in money wages would, ceteris paribus, restore a correct relative price between 'bonds' and labour services. But since we are in a general equilibrium model, this would clearly not achieve the appropriate price ratios between 'bonds' and the other commodities of the model. Moreover, the Pigou effect — the direct effect on aggregate expenditure of a change in the value of the nominal money stock — is irrelevant in this setting. For, as we have seen, Keynes' diagnosis of the malady is that relative prices are 'wrong'; and, if this is the case, an all-round deflation will not help. A priori it could only work if it affected relative prices, i.e. if it lowers the rate of interest relative to the money wage rate. This is possible since the rate of interest has the highest ranking in terms of velocity among the set of prices in Keynes' short period model. But now we are really talking about the Keynes' wealth effect, i.e. the effect on aggregate consumption of changes in the rate of interest. Leijonhufvud's dismissal of the Pigou effect is very neat.

NOTES

4   Formally, given a set of commodities $X_1, X_2, \ldots, X_n$, we consider the relation $X_i \, E \, X_j$ to be an exchange relation which is non-empty and reflexive. In a barter economy, the relation is transitive for all i and j. In a pure money economy, the relationship is non-transitive and holds only when the ith commodity is money.

5   In order to clarify this matter it is useful to make the following distinctions.

$$\sum_{i}^{m} p_i q_i \quad = \sum_{j}^{n} w_j \, z_j \qquad (1)$$

$$\sum_{i}^{m} p_i^e \, q_i^e \quad = \sum_{j}^{n} w_j \, z_j \qquad (2)$$

$$\sum_{i}^{m} p_i^* \, q_i^* \quad = \sum_{j}^{n} w_j^* \, z_j^* \qquad (3)$$

where $i = 1, \ldots, m$; $j = m + 1, \ldots, n$, p_i, p_i^e, p_i^* are the actual, expected and equilibrium price of the ith commodity: q_i, q_i^e q_i^* are the respective excess demands: w_j, w_j^e and w_j^* are the actual, expected and equilibrium price of the jth productive service and z_j, z_j^e and z_j^* are the respective excess supplies.

Equation (1) states that the sum of the actual value of the excess demands for commodities in the economy is equal to the sum of the actual values of the excess supplies of factor services at any actual set of prices of goods and factor services. Equation (2) states that the sum of the value of the planned excess demand for goods by transactors at expected prices is equal to the sum of the value of the actual excess supply of factor services at the actual set of factor prices. Equation (3) states that in a full equilibrium of the system, the sum of the value of the excess demand for commodities is equal to the sum of the value of the excess supply of factor services at a set of prices which guarantees simultaneous equilibrium in all markets. Since the situation relates to the short run we add variables to the R.H.S. of each equation corresponding to the actual, expected and equilibrium level of profits. We also assume that all profits are distributed as incomes to households.

Equation (3) corresponds to Clower's notional relationships. Equations (1) and (2) correspond to his actual relationships on the assumption that the plans which transactors make on the basis of their actual incomes can always be executed in a manner which does not violate the constraint which is imposed by the actual level of aggregate incomes.

In a full equilibrium of the system, all three equations hold simultaneously. Actual, expected and equilibrium values are then identical. (The L.H.S. of all three equations are equal therefore their R.H.S. are also equal.) However, in disequilibrium, these equations do not hold simultaneously since actual, expected and market clearing values are different. Specifically, Walras' Law does not hold as between notional and effective excess demands (the L.H.S. of (3) and (1) are unequal), i.e. the sum of the value of the actual excess demand for goods is not equal to the sum of the equilibrium excess demands because actual factor incomes are not equal to their equilibrium value.

III The Income Expenditure Model and the Economics of Keynes

All this is clearly very exciting. For it lays to rest one's uneasy feeling that somehow our basic model for explaining short-run fluctuations is, unlike the Walrasian or Marshallian theory, not anchored in the fundamentals of our discipline. In the received interpretation there appear to be too many elements of theoretical adhocery. But it is now clear that short-run macro theory does have an impeccable lineage. What is more this interpretation of Keynes' theory opens up new vistas not only in the realm of pure theory but in the field of the analysis of economies which are on-going concerns.

And yet, one does detect signs of a rather uneasy response to the work of Clower and Leijonhufvud. One could argue that it is early days yet: Leijonhufvud's book appeared in 1968. On the other hand Clower's seminal paper (5) has been available for at least five years. Considering the general furore and excitement which has immediately surrounded lesser contributions, one is led to speculate on why this is the case.

(i)   One possible reason is that if the Clower-Leijonhufvud interpretation of Keynes' theory is correct, many eminent economists may feel uncomfortable. To paraphrase Johnson's review which appeared in Encounter (16): both Milton Friedman and Mrs. Robinson can commend Leijonhufvud's book to their students with a fair conscience; Paul Samuelson, leader of the American Keynesian tradition, will find it embarrassing to do so. Although it appears rather odd that Professor Johnson should put Professors Friedman and Robinson in the same box, there is something in this. It is often said that the progress of science depends upon the death or at any rate the retirement of professors.

(ii) Secondly, there is the fact that the work of Clower and Leijonhufvud is not as mathematically elegant as many of their more conceptually and empirically empty competitors. And regrettably the average level of technical expertise in the profession is as yet not sufficiently high to drive to zero the quasi-rents from the manipulation of models which make no new conceptual or empirical advance. Too often economists shy away from the analysis of real problems because they are not readily amenable to treatment by the available set of techniques. It is also frequently forgotten that specification of the framework and the conceptual basis of the problem which is to be analysed is a prerequisite for good model building.

(iii) But a third and perhaps more important reason for the observed unease, and this applies specifically to the work of Leijonhufvud, is the insistent attack throughout his book upon the income expenditure model (which we may take to mean the Hicks-Hansen apparatus and its elaboration at the hands of Modigliani (24, 25) and others) as a framework within which to express and develop the central ideas of the General Theory.

Now when all the esoteric frills are ignored, I suspect that when the work-a-day economist is faced with a real world problem he instinctively uses one or more of three basic models. He uses the supply and demand apparatus for the determination of relative prices, the income expenditure model to handle short-run stabilisation problems, and some amalgam of the Ricardo-Marx-Solow-Harrod growth models with a dash of Ramsey to analyse questions of long run accumulation. If this is the case, then Leijonhufvud is asking the economist to throw away a substantial part of his analytical equipment and, since in his book he offers no alternative formal apparatus to take its place, this is asking rather a lot. For, as Kuhn (21) has shown, a scientific community does not jettison an established analytical framework until it is offered an alternative within which it can not only handle its standard problems, but also deal with important problems which had to be regarded as anomalies from the standpoint of the existing framework. Fortunately, I think it is possible to show that Keynes' major theoretical insights can be conveyed within the context of the income expenditure model.

On my reading of this book, Leijonhufvud considers that the

income expenditure model departs from Keynes' model in three major respects. The first is the general 'elasticity' pessimism of the income expenditure model. The second is the different aggregative structure of the models. The third concerns the differences in the rationalisations of the functional relationships of the models.

iii(a)   Under the heading of elasticity pessimism come the assumptions about interest inelastic aggregate expenditure functions and the notion of the liquidity trap. Of a somewhat different but not unrelated nature are the assumptions about money illusion and the institutional rigidity of money wages. Here it is necessary to distinguish between the income expenditure <u>model</u> and the income expenditure <u>theorists</u>. It is clear that all these assumptions have been made by income expenditure theorists. But these assumptions are not inherent in the formal structure of the model[6]. The real issue is why the solution to this short period model (in the sense of Marshall and Hicks) is not uniquely one of full-employment. One answer, and, as it turns out, a theoretically trivial answer which runs in terms of liquidity traps, absolute rigidity of money wage rates, etc., has been given by the income expenditure theorists. The other.has been given by Clower and Leijonhufvud. I therefore consider that their work has provided a theoretically satisfactory <u>basis</u> for a proof of the possibility of an under-employment solution to the income expenditure model.

iii(b)   Consider next the different aggregative structures of the models. Both contain five goods: consumer goods, investment goods, labour, money and bonds. But both solve for three relative prices only. For this to be admissible, one of the goods must be eliminated by assimilating it into another. Leijonhufvud claims that by employing an aggregate production function the income expenditure model assimilates consumer goods to capital goods. In contrast Keynes assimilates bonds to capital goods.

An aggregation procedure reflects the purpose of the theorist. The procedure of the income expenditure theorists, which implies a distinction between physical and financial assets, reflects a concern with the effect on these assets of changes in the aggregate price level – a variable which is not even defined in Keynes' model. For Keynes the characteristic property of 'bonds' and capital goods is the similar way in which they are affected by changes in the rate of interest.

Hence what dominates his aggregation procedure with respect to assets is their differentiation along the maturity spectrum. From the standpoint of exegesis, Leijonhufvud is partially correct. His statement concerning the aggregation procedure in the income expenditure model is fully applicable to the work of later theorists only. For instance, in "Mr. Keynes and the Classics" (11a) Hicks distinguished between investment goods and consumer goods and wrote down separate production functions for them. His five commodity model has four relative prices: the price of consumer goods, the price of investment goods, the wage rate and the rate of interest. Aggregate income is simply defined as the sum of incomes earned in the consumer goods and investment goods industries.

Be that as it may, if one considers that Keynes' basic and relevant result is the income constrained process that is initiated by some disturbance which produces a discrepancy between plans to save and plans to invest at the initial set of asset prices, the one commodity version of the income expenditure model will suffice. Keynes' analysis was conducted in terms of the relative spot prices of bonds, consumer goods, money and labour services. In the income expenditure model, the analysis needs to be conducted in terms of the expected price of the future commodity in terms of the present commodity set against the money rate of interest and the money wage rate.

A careful reading of his book shows that Leijonhufvud is aware of this, but in my view he regrettably plays it down. His legitimate quarrel is with the rationalisation of the under-employment solution to the income expenditure model provided by a distinguished line of economists including Hicks; it is not with the model as such[7].

iii(c) Finally, there is the question of differences in the rationalisation of the functional relationships of Keynes' theory.

Until now, the rationalisations of Keynes' key functional relationships which have been offered by Keynesians including Keynes himself, have been unsatisfactory from the standpoint of pure theory. Let us consider two examples: the consumption function and the demand for money function.

In his 1937 Q.J.E. article, Keynes (20) pointed out that his consumption function in which planned consumption depends on actual income (and to a lesser extent on the rate of interest) was one of the most important of his theoretical innovations. Yet he had simply postulated its existence on terms of two unexplored psychological 'laws'. The Keynesian consumption function has been attacked on two grounds.

First it is supposed to be ad hoc and not rooted in the fundamentals of value theory inasmuch as the demand functions of general equilibrium theory, which are the outcome of a constrained optimisation problem, contain prices of goods and factors as their arguments. Logically, they do not contain income even though they may contain initial endowments[8]. However, once we grasp the Clower interpretation of Keynes' theory, the theoretical rationale of the dependence of planned consumption on actual incomes becomes clear. In a money economy, plans to buy are usually contingent on the successful execution of plans to sell. For example, the worker usually has to sell his labour services for money before he can implement his plans to buy goods. But this means that at a wrong set of relative prices, notional and actual incomes diverge, in which case actual incomes are what determine expenditure even though normal incomes do play a role inasmuch as it is the wealth holders' view that the value of their assets is not perfectly liquid, which accounts for the emergence of the divergence between actual and notional incomes. Unless the system is in a full equilibrium, actual incomes do legitimately enter into demand functions together with prices and realised incomes do impose a binding constraint on planned expenditure.

The second ground of the attack is that given the assumption of a fixed capital stock, Keynes ignored the effect of wealth upon aggregate consumption, wealth being defined as the net worth of the private sector. We have already seen that the implied Pigou effect is irrelevant in the context of Keynes' analysis. Moreover, there is a wealth effect in the General Theory according to which aggregate consumption is inversely related to the rate of interest.

The first point to notice is that whether a fall or a rise in interest rates makes an asset holder better or worse off depends on the relationship between the life of the asset and the encashment schedule which is implied by the asset holder's consumption plan. Suppose that an individual plans to hold stocks of bonds re-investing the interest until a date in the future at which, given his consumption plan, everything will be encashed. A fall in the current interest rate increases the present value of these assets but thereafter their value grows more slowly. A rise in the current interest rate reduces the present value of the assets but thereafter their value grows more quickly. This being the case there is some date at which the value of these assets is the same irrespective of whether the current interest rate has fallen or risen[9]. The asset holder is thus better off, worse off or unaffected by a change in the rate of interest according to whether his consumption plan requires that the asset be encashed before, at or after this specific date in the future.

Secondly, it has to be shown that the aggregate wealth effect of a change in the rate of interest can be non-zero. For it has been argued that a change in the rate of interest as such does nothing to alter the real transformation possibilities which are open to society. Consequently, if households maximise well ordered utility functions and if, as is not often pointed out in the context, they have full information concerning transformation possibilities and are infinitely lived, then a wealth effect cannot exist in the absence of some sort of illusion. There are distribution effects, but these cancel out in the aggregate if all individuals have linear and identical Engel curves and/or if households are infinitely lived. Thus at the aggregate level changes in the rate of interest generate substitution effects only. Concerning substitution effects, Leijonhufvud argues that Keynes' model can be taken to assume a strict complementarity between present and future consumption so that substitution effects are zero. (If complementarity is not strict, substitution effects are assumed to be small enough to be neglected.) Concerning income effects, we have already seen that the Keynesian theory assumes that asset holders are rational but that they are neither fully informed nor infinitely lived. The representative asset holder in Keynes' theory who is faced with uncertainty about future bond prices, is in a phase of his life cycle and is holding a portfolio of bonds whose date to maturity is longer than the encashment schedule implied by his consumption plan. Consequently, a fall (rise) in the rate of interest makes him better (worse) off. Hence, viewed as the effect on the consumption possibilities of those who own the titles to the economy's capital stock, wealth as perceived by them is affected by a change in the rate of interest. Viewed as the maximum level of production which the existing transformation possibilities permit, wealth is unchanged.

This question of the wealth effects of changes in the rate of interest is not necessarily central to the proof of the possibility of

Keynes' unemployment state. Nevertheless it brings into relief the difference between the economics of Keynes and Neo-Classical economics. The Neo-Classical proposition is that since rational and fully informed transactors perceive transformation possibilities correctly, the wealth effect of a change in interest rates is zero. In contrast the Keynesian contention that such wealth effects are non-zero can be taken to imply that, in a disequilibrium of the whole system, rational agents do not perceive transformation possibilities correctly (36). Indeed this is an essential property of a disequilibrium situation. In a depression, transactors behave as if they are too poor to demand the output which the economy is capable of producing. In an inflation, they behave as if they consider that their real income is adequate to purchase more goods and services than the system can actually produce.

Leijonhufvud's price theoretic rationalisation of the Keynes wealth effect may turn out to be controversial. But it is a tour de force.

Consider now the demand for money. Clower's work has provided a basis for an intellectually satisfactory statement of the essential properties of a money economy. Money is the only commodity which is by social convention accepted in all markets and this makes it the means of payment. This seems to me to provide the necessary backdrop to the work of Tobin (33) and Baumol (4), who treat the transaction demand as a problem in inventory theory. Moreover, the role of money as the most liquid asset in the system and its consequent superiority in some situations as a store of value is predicated upon the convention which establishes it as means of payment.

In his classic paper Tobin (34) showed that the assumption of inelastic expectations which is the basis of Keynes' speculative motive, is not necessary to derive the asset demand for money. He derives it by invoking the precautionary motive which requires that risk averting asset holders should diversify portfolios, a derivation which is consistent with unity elasticity of expectations. However, it should be pointed out that Keynes' theory of the asset demand is a fusion of both the precautionary and the speculative motives. Moreover, Keynes' 'money' contains many of the short assets on the maturity spectrum which the current portfolio selection literature regards as 'bonds' and among which its asset holders are choosing as against money. There is no right way of defining variables; how they are defined depends on the problem in hand. Thus it is not a relevant criticism of Keynes' theory to say that given the existence of assets with different dates to maturity, a fall in the rate of interest might simply induce asset holders to move to the shorter end of the maturity spectrum without necessarily increasing their holdings of cash. For, given his definition of 'money', what Keynes was attempting to establish is that any such aggregate shift would have implications for capital formation, output and employment. Moreover, just as the transactions demand (the use of money as means of payment) is the key element in his explanation of the failure to co-ordinate decisions to demand and supply labour, it is the speculative motive (the use of money as a store of values) based as it is on the assumption of inelastic expectations which is responsible for the failure of the interest rate to fall sufficiently to equate savings and investment without a contraction in employment and output.

This brings into relief an important aspect of Keynesian monetary theory. For, while it is clear that in the case of the transactions demand money must be defined as means of payment, the means of payment being the asset(s) with the lowest transactions cost, the position is different when the asset demand is also involved. For instance, in a world of many assets with varying dates to maturity, Keynes' 'money' is representative of assets with a low interest elasticity of present value, while 'bonds' are representative of assets with a high interest elasticity of present value, the borderline between those assets which are to be regarded as 'money' and those which are to be regarded as 'bonds' being determined by the analytical problem in hand. But this really means that the variability in velocity which the existence of the asset demand implies is not merely a question of the transfer of cash between 'active' and 'idle' balances. The transfer which occurs in periods of changing expectations or in response to monetary policy also involves a change in the composition and the definition of 'money'. This might very well be a fruitful angle from which to appraise the concern of Radcliffe (30a) with the problem of liquidity.

(iv) One final reason for the observed unease is that Leijonhufvud's work might be interpreted as an attempt to demonstrate that Keynes was an early precursor of Milton Friedman. On this view,

Leijonhufvud's sharp distinction between Keynes and the Keynesians, his insistent attack upon the income expenditure model and his assessment of the views of Keynes, Friedman and the income expenditure theorists concerning the causes of the great depression (22a) can be regarded as part of the endeavour to legitimise the monetarist counter-revolution. The crucial proposition is that for Keynes and Friedman money matters, whereas for the Keynesians money does not matter.

Now, although money does matter in the Keynesian system, it is not the case that Keynes was a founding father of monetarism. Moreover, it is well known that except in the most vulgar versions of Keynesianism, Keynesians have not generally held that money does not matter. Every exposition of the Keynesian model which an undergraduate encounters in serious textbooks or in the literature contains some sort of monetary sector. Moreover, whatever may be the differences between Keynesian economics and the economics of Keynes, they are sui generis. The same cannot be said about the economics of Keynes and that of the monetarists.

The most sophisticated version of the monetarist model appears to consist of the following elements. There is a stock demand function for real money balances which has as arguments permanent income and the actual rate of interest, rather than the spread between the actual and the expected rate of interest as the Liquidity Preference theory would lead us to expect. An extrapolative expectations equation connects permanent income to actual income. A similar extrapolative equation governs the adjustment of actual money stocks to their desired level. The nominal stock of money is exogenously determined and a market clearing condition closes the system. The model may be solved to obtain an equation with either real money balances or the level of money income as the dependent variable. Income and the rate of interest (the latter variable is sometimes excluded) are assumed to be exogenous in the money equation. Similarly the stock of money is assumed to be independent of the level of income in the income equation [10].

Now it is rather strange that in the money equation we are expected to assume that actual real money balances can be identified with the demand for money, whereas in the income equation the nominal values of these same balances are to be identified with the supply. Furthermore, it cannot be said that the income equation constitutes a satisfactory explanation of the determination of the level of money income. For we are not given a model which is distinct from that of Keynes or the Keynesians and which includes an explicit mechanism whereby the effects of a change in the stock of money are transmitted to the level of income. We are simply told that, contrary to what was assumed by Keynes, the empirical evidence shows that the elasticity of substitution between bonds and money is low whereas that between goods and money is high. Moreover, we are not told how a change in money income consequent on a change in the money stock decomposes into a change in output and a change in prices, or for that matter into a change in consumption and a change in investment. But we do need to have these matters spelt out and the issue cannot be avoided by appealing to the distinction between Marshallian and Walrasian methods of analysis. The Marshallian method requires that one is clear about one's underlying general theory and in partial analysis one must specify explicitly what is being impounded under the ceteris paribus clause. Thus the Classical assumption of a full employment level of income generates the result that a change in the money supply will only result in a change in the aggregate price level. Under the extreme 'Keynesian' assumption of zero velocity of the prices of goods within the unit period, the corresponding response is a change in real output only. Under less stringent assumptions than either of these two extremes, theorists in the Keynesian tradition have attempted to divide the resulting change between price and output. Until very recently the monetarists have refused to attempt such a division and have thus avoided the articulation of a general model. We have been asked instead to accept the rather dubious positivist principle that the sole relevant test of a theory is its ability to predict much from little. Their approach is then justified by appealing to the observation that the correlation between changes in money income and lagged or contemporaneous changes in the money supply is greater than that between changes in money income and changes in autonomous expenditure. Even if we were to ignore the fact that these results have been challenged in the literature and even if we did not question the view of the Keynesian theory which the test procedure implies, their results do not prove that changes in the money stock rather than changes in autonomous expenditure are the cause of changes in income. For in a money economy, in order to effect an increase in planned expenditure, there must usually be a prior increase in the demand for money provided that, before the change, the actual and desired levels of the money holdings of the relevant transactors are equal. If the supply of money is increased to meet the demand, we would then observe that an increase in money balances precedes the increase in income even if the increase in income is the result of an increase in autonomous expenditures. Moreover, if the increase in transactions balances is partly brought about by a rise in the rate of interest as of a given stock of money, we may also find that a rise in the rate of interest precedes changes in the level of income. In any event, if the proposition that we can predict changes in money income from changes in the supply of money is to make analytical sense, not only do we require that changes in the supply of money be exogenous and that the money commodities be capable of unambiguous and invariant definitions, but we also require that the relationship between changes in the money supply and changes in income be shown under clearly stated assumptions to be the reduced form of some underlying model. Prediction is then possible under conditions of unchanged structure. And if, as it turns out to be the case, the underlying model is seen to be either the familiar textbook Keynesian or Classical models or some amalgam of them, one is led to wonder what the fuss is all about.

Alternatively, we may take the view that what the monetarists have attempted to provide is a theory and some estimates of the parameters of the demand function for money.

Judged as a theory of the demand for money, Friedman's re-statement of the Quantity Theory (9) is, as Patinkin (28) has pointed out, simply a more elegant statement of Keynes' liquidity preference hypothesis. However, at another level, the monetarists have not provided an intellectually satisfactory rationalisation of the existence of this demand function. They have not invoked a Keynesian type rationalisation, but have instead maintained that the demand for money is to be explained in exactly the same way as the demand for any other commodity. Thus money is like any other commodity even though it is defined to be 'a temporary abode of purchasing power'. It therefore appears as if the theory deals with a barter economy which is in a full equilibrium. It does not seem as if we are in a monetary economy which is an on-going concern. We may, however, take the view that what they have attempted to do is to estimate the parameters of the demand function for money in a

Keynesian model and that their major conclusion is that the demand function for money is stable. Several objections to this work have been made in the literature and we will not discuss them all[11]. The following appear to be decisive.

The data which are used in these studies of the aggregate demand for money are the actual and not the desired stock of money. But the actual stock of nominal money balances is not a decision variable for all transactors taken together. Of course it is assumed that the market clears from period to period so that the actual stock of money satisfies the demand and supply equations simultaneously. But then it can be plausibly argued that the supply function contains as arguments the same explanatory variables as are used in the demand function. This being the case, the question of whether a model has been specified which allows the demand function to be identified would then arise. It could be argued that a demand function has been identified in the data inasmuch as there is prior information that the authorities vary the money supply to meet the needs of trade or to peg bond prices. But in that case, monetarist policy conclusions concerning the monetary authority's ability to control the money supply, which are predicated upon their empirical findings, are suspect. For in this setting, the observed stability in velocity would simply be a reflection of the volatility of supply. It yields no information on how velocity would behave in the face of any attempt to control the supply of the money commodities which then happen to be in being. Neither does it tell us how the economy would use its undoubted ability to create money substitutes if, feasible changes in velocity given, the government refused over a given period of time to provide money to meet the needs of trade.

NOTES

6 Not only are such assumptions not inherent in the formal structure of the income expenditure model but, as Leijonhufvud reminds us, Keynes never made them. For one thing, it is hardly possible to find a statement in the General Theory to the effect that money wages are rigid. Again, Keynes was far more concerned with the shifts in the liquidity preference function which are associated with the crumbling of normal or expected values as a disequilibrium process gets under way, than with

postulating an infinite elasticity of the liquidity preference function with respect to the actual rate of interest as of a given expected interest rate. Further, Keynes never postulated that expenditure functions are interest inelastic with an elasticity approaching zero. Although he did not carry out any empirical work on this matter and was not very charitable to Tinbergen's work in this area, Keynes was a believer in the efficacy of the rate of interest and was a life-long advocate of low long rates. What he did maintain was that in the conditions of the 1930's, only a monetary policy à outrance could get long rates down to the appropriate level and, given the banking conventions and institutional arrangements then in being, central banks were unlikely to pursue such a policy.

It should be pointed out that recent empirical studies (12, 35) in which the relevant hypotheses and the underlying lag structures are carefully specified suggest that, contrary to the proposition of the income expenditure theorists, expenditure functions <u>are</u> interest elastic.

7   This does not mean that the income expenditure model is necessarily an appropriate framework for the analysis of all the questions of Keynesian exegesis. Neither is its conventional version devoid of blemishes or traps which usually ensnare the unwary. For one thing, as we shall show below, the demand function for money which the model contains must be amended if we are to discuss problems of disequilibrium dynamics such as the determination of short run movements in the rate of interest. Another related matter has been pointed out by Mundell (25). It is usually incorrectly assumed that because the effect upon aggregate supply of a change in investment can be ignored in the short period of the model, the corresponding effects on the price of assets and the composition of portfolios can also be ignored. Again since it distinguishes between physical and monetary assets, the usual version of the model is under-determined unless an equation in variables such as the expected rate of change of the aggregate price level is added to connect the money and the real rate of interest.

8   It is not even clear why the consumption functions which are generated in the class of normal income hypotheses and which are supposed to be anchored in the theory of optimising behaviour should have expected incomes rather than an inter-temporal vector of prices as their arguments.

9   An asset is acquired at $t = 0$ and held until some date t, interest being re-invested. Write r_0 for the initial rate of interest and r_1 for a rise and r_1' for a fall in the rate of interest at the beginning of period $t = 1$. Given a rise in the rate of interest to r_1, the value of assets at date t is given by

$$(r_0/r_1 + r_0) \ (1 + r_1)^{t-1} \qquad\qquad (1)$$

The rise in the rate of interest lowers the expression in the first parenthesis but increases the expression in the second parenthesis. Conversely, a fall in the rate of interest gives the value of assets at date t as

$$(r_0/r_1' + r_0) (1 + r_1')^{t-1} \qquad (2)$$

The fall in the rate of interest raises the expression in the first parenthesis but lowers the expression in the second parenthesis. Solving (1) and (2), we can find some

$$t = \theta = \log\left(\frac{r_1}{r_1'}\right) \Big/ \frac{\log(1 + r_1)}{\log(1 + r_1')}$$

at which date the effect of the capital gain or loss is exactly offset by the differing rates of accumulation.

The question is discussed further in Matthews (23).

10 The model may be written down formally as follows:

$$M_t^* = \alpha + \beta Y_t^e + \gamma r_t$$

$$Y_t^e = \lambda Y_t + (1 - \lambda) Y_{t-1}^e, \qquad 0 < \lambda < 1$$

$$M_t = \theta M_t^* + (1 - \theta) M_{t-1} + u_t, \qquad 0 < \theta < 1$$

M_t^* is the desired stock of real cash balances in period t, M_t is the actual stock of money in period t, r_t is the actual rate of interest in period t, Y_t is the actual level of income at the end of period t, Y_t^e is the expected level of income at the beginning of period t, λ is the proportion by which the level of income expected at the end of period t is revised in the light of observed discrepancies between actual income at the beginning of period t and expected income at the end of period $t - 1$, θ is the proportion by which actual real balances are assumed to approach their desired level within the unit period, and u_t is a random disturbance term.

These equations may be solved to obtain:

$$M_t = \alpha\theta\lambda + \beta\theta\lambda Y_t + \gamma\theta r_t - [\gamma\theta(1-\lambda)] r_{t-1}$$

$$+ (2 - \theta - \lambda) M_{t-1} - [(1 - \theta)(1 - \lambda)] M_{t-2} + v_t$$

and

$$Y_t = \frac{1}{\beta\theta\lambda} M_t - \frac{\alpha}{\beta} - \frac{\gamma}{\beta\lambda} r_t + \frac{\gamma(1-\lambda)}{\beta\lambda} r_{t-1}$$

$$- \frac{(2-\theta-\lambda)}{\beta\theta\lambda} M_{t-1} + \frac{(1-\theta)(1-\lambda)}{\beta\theta\lambda} M_{t-2} + w_t$$

11 A succinct statement of many of these objections is to be found
   in (17, 4a).

IV A Reappraisal of the Keynesian Theory of Interest

In this section, we propose to re-examine the question of the logical validity of the explanation of short run movements in the interest rate which is based on the Liquidity Preference theory.

Such a re-examination is necessary for three reasons. Firstly, although their work is relevant to it, such a reappraisal has not been attempted by Clower and Leijonhufvud. Secondly, the alleged inadequacy in the Liquidity Preference theory of interest rates has, at any rate by implication, been used to cast doubt on Keynes' short period employment theory in which the notion of liquidity preference plays a crucial role. Finally, it enables us to provide an important illustration of our contention, that Keynes' crucial propositions can be expounded and analysed within the framework of the income expenditure model[12].

We assume an n commodity model. There are n−2 goods and it is assumed that the conditions are satisfied under which they can be treated either as a composite commodity called output, or can be composited into two commodities, namely capital goods and consumer goods. (In the former case the commodity is either consumed or is transmogrified into capital goods.) The n−1th commodity is a bond to perpetuity and, except for the case of consumption loans, is issued by firms and held by households as an asset. These bonds are the financial instruments which correspond to the stock of capital goods. The nth commodity is fiat money, the stock of which is assumed to be fixed by the monetary authorities. The analysis is conducted within the framework of one Hicksian week during which some decision variables are assumed to be unalterable while others are the subject of current choice. The 'week' is defined in terms of the equality of savings and investment. Its calendar date counterpart is "the time it takes the multiplier to work itself out"[13]. The wage contract is assumed to be fixed at the end of the previous period so that the money wage rate is not a decision variable within the current period. The money price level of commodities is variable subject to the constraint which is imposed by the fixed money wage rate. The rate of interest is the highest ranked price in terms of velocity within the unit period. The permissible range of variations in its level is given by the assumption of inelastic long run expectations which underlies the liquidity preference schedule.

The excess demand functions which correspond to the three commodities, goods, bonds, and money, may be written as follows:

$$Y_t - C(Y_{t-i}, r_t) - I(Y_{t-i}, r_t) = 0 \qquad (1)$$

$$rP.H(Y_{t-i}, \frac{1}{r_t}) - rP.J(Y_{t-i}, \frac{1}{r_t}) = 0 \qquad (2)$$

$$P.L(Y_{t-i}, r_t) - M^O = 0 \qquad (3a)$$

$$P.L(C_t, I_t, r_t) - M^O = 0 \qquad (3b)$$

where Y, C, I and r are income, consumption, investment and the rate of interest, M^O is the total stock of nominal money and P is a fixed weight index of the money prices P_1, P_2, ... , P_n. Although the price level is not a constant within the unit period, we have not included the value of real cash balances $(\frac{M^O}{P})$ in any of these functions. Since the rate of interest is the highest ranked price in terms of velocity within the unit period, the exclusion of $(\frac{M^O}{P})$ does not affect our qualitative conclusions. In any case, we have already seen that the cash balance effect is irrelevant to the problem situation of Keynes' theory. We shall call the system consisting of equations (1), (2) and (3a) Model I and that consisting of Equations (1), (2) and (3b) Model II. The equations of the labour market are omitted since we are not immediately concerned with the level of employment. However, since we make the assumptions of a given nominal wage rate within the unit period and unemployed resources, the systems represented by Models I and II are to be regarded as reduced forms conditional on the level at which the nominal stock of money and the money wage rate are set.

Equation (3b) is the demand function for money which is appropriate to disequilibrium analysis. It makes the transactions demand depend on the parameters of planned spending rather than on the realised level of output. If the transaction demand is made to depend on the short run expenditure function which has a positive intercept and a slope which is less than unity, when the expenditure function shifts because of an autonomous increase in some component of planned spending, the demand for money function also shifts[14]. This shift in the demand for money function reflects the fact that in a money economy in order to effect an increase in planned expenditure there must be a prior increase in the demand for the intermediary commodity, provided that before the change actual and desired levels of money holdings of the relevant transactors are equal. This is lost sight of when the transactions demand is made to depend on actual output, since, in that case, a change in planned expenditure does not affect the demand for money until there is an induced change in the level of output. If we are merely interested in analysing situations in which the goods market is in equilibrium then it does not matter whether the transactions demand for money is made to depend on the level of output or on the parameters of planned expenditure. However, if we wish to analyse states of disequilibrium in the goods market, the demand function for money must be chosen appropriately.

Given this framework, the two theories of short run movements in the interest rate which we wish to discuss are the Liquidity Preference theory which states that the rate of interest changes if and only if the excess demand for money is non-zero, and the Loanable Funds theory which states that the rate of interest changes if and only if the excess demand for bonds is non-zero. That is

$$\frac{\partial r}{\partial t} = q_M(p_1, p_2, \dots, p_n) \text{ is the L.P. theory, and}$$

$$\frac{\partial r}{\partial t} = q_B(p_1, p_2, \dots, p_n) \text{ is the L.F. theory.}$$

All are agreed that a definition according to which the L.P. theory states that the rate of interest is determined by the demand for and supply of money and the L.F. theory states that it is determined by the demand for and supply of bonds, is unsatisfactory. In a general equilibrium system the price of any given commodity is determined by the complete set of demand and supply relationships and not by a particular sub-set.

Following Hicks' classic demonstration (11), it is generally agreed that when the market for goods is in equilibrium the Liquidity

Preference and Loanable Funds theories are equivalent, since in such a situation excess demand for (supply of) money implies excess supply of (demand of) securities. In terms of our models, so long as equation (1) is satisfied, any values of the variables which satisfy (3a) or (3b) must also satisfy (2).

As long as the analysis is confined to states of equilibrium in the goods market the equivalence of the two theories is not upset by the observation that the one deals with the supply and demand for stocks whereas the other deals with the demand and supply of flows. The stock theory can be converted into a flow theory since the excess demand for a stock, i.e. the planned change in the level of a stock between two dates divided by the length of the period, is equivalent to the excess demand for a flow.

However, when there is disequilibrium in the goods market, there is considerable disagreement among theorists about which theory provides the more satisfactory explanation of the behaviour of the interest rate. The prevalent view seems to be that the two theories are different in the sense that they imply different adjustment processes in the same market. Some contributors conclude (not necessarily from the same reasoning) that the L.F. theory is superior, while others are of the opposite opinion.

Let us examine the two cases around which much of the debate in the literature has been centred. In the one, equilibrium is disturbed by a change in the marginal efficiency of capital; in the other it is disturbed by a change in liquidity preference.

(i)   Suppose that, starting from a position of equilibrium, there is an exogenous change in the state of long term expectations which affects the marginal efficiency of capital and causes an increase in planned investment expenditures. (Exactly the same analysis holds for an autonomous change in planned savings which leaves undisturbed the ratio in which individuals desire to hold bonds and money which is held as an asset.) With the demand function for money written as in (3a), the L.P. theory implies that the rate of interest cannot change until there is a change in the level of output. As has been pointed out, Keynes' procedure in the General Theory is to assume that given the increase in investment, output adjusts immediately to satisfy equation (1). Income having changed, the increased demand for transactions balances puts upward pressure on the interest rate. This means that in equation (1) income enters without a lag but enters with a one-period lag into equation (3a).

Loanable funds theorists have objected to this procedure on the grounds that it is unrealistic to assume what it implies, namely, that decisions about the level and composition of output are completed more quickly than decisions about the composition of assets. They contend that the opposite assumption is more reasonable. Consequently, they postulate a Robertsonian lag in the consumption function but no lag in the money demand function, i.e. i is set equal to unity in equation (1) and set equal to zero in equation (3a).

Now consider again a shift in the investment function. Investors finance the increased investment by a sale of bonds in the market for new issues. This excess demand for commodities is accompanied by an excess supply of securities which, according to the L.F. theory, forces up the rate of interest. But the level of income has not altered. Hence according to (3a), the excess demand for money is zero. Therefore, according to the L.P. theory, the rate of interest is unchanged in the current period. Thus the L.P. theory seems to say that the rate of interest remains unchanged when the excess demand for loans is non-zero.

What we now wish to show is that it is possible to maintain the L.P. theory in the presence of a lagged consumption function, with or without a Lundberg lag, and without the proposition implied in (3a) that a shift in some parameter of planned spending influences the rate of interest only through a change in output. To do this all we need to do is give up equation (3a) and replace it by (3b), i.e. we make the transaction demand for money depend on the parameters of planned expenditure rather than on the level of output.

Consider again an equilibrium situation which is disturbed by a plan to increase investment. In a money economy, this can only be effected through the use of money. Assuming that there is not simultaneously a reduction in liquidity preference, investors obtain the requisite money balances by issuing new bonds which drives up the rate of interest, persuading asset holders to substitute bonds for money in their portfolios. The rate of interest therefore rises in the face of an excess demand for money, as predicted by the Liquidity Preference theory, and in the face of an excess supply of bonds, as predicted by the Loanable Funds theory. Let us restate the argument. In terms of Walras' Law, which in this context is the statement $X_g + X_b + X_m = 0$, the situation may be written as $X_g = -X_b$ since, given the usual form of the excess demand function for money in (3a), $X_m = 0$, where X_g, X_b and X_m are the values of the excess demand for goods, bonds and money respectively. However, as we have already argued, Walras' Law does not hold in such a situation. It is only in a barter economy (or in a mixed money and barter economy) that bonds can be directly exchanged for goods. In a pure money economy (and the literature deals with either pure barter or pure money economies) two transactions are involved, an exchange of bonds for money and then an exchange of money for goods, i.e. we have $X_M = -X_b$ in the first instance and then $-X_m = X_g$, where X_M is the excess demand for money in the income constraint and X_m is the excess demand for money in the expenditure constraint[15]. The Liquidity Preference theory and the Loanable Funds theory both predict a rise in the rate of interest as a result of the exchange of bonds for money.

Whether the rate of interest remains at this new higher level at the end of the period or reverts to the level it stood at the beginning of the period depends on what we assume to happen when the money acquired by investors is exchanged for capital goods, i.e. what is the consequence for the interest rate of the second transaction $X_g = -X_m$?

In the literature, most theorists assume that within the period in which it has taken place, the increased demand for capital goods is met from a passive decumulation of inventories. This follows from the postulate of a Lundberg lag such that $Z_t = Y_{t-1}$ and $Y_t = Z_t - V_t$ where Z is output, Y is demand and V is the change in inventories which are to be regarded as passive investment. The unexpected increase in the sales of stockholders means that their actual income exceeds their expected income. Invoking the dual decision hypothesis we may then say that a revision of their planned expenditure is now required. But since expenditure on goods cannot be altered until the following period ($i \neq 0$ in equation (1)), the only decision which these passive investors can take concerns the composition of their portfolios. They may take the opportunity presented by the unintended accretion of cash balances to retire outstanding debt by an amount equal to the bond creation of active investors re-issuing it at the beginning of the next period to finance their increased expenditure. Alternatively, they may voluntarily decide to hold the additional cash in anticipation of their increased expenditure in the subsequent period. Which behaviour will be optimal depends on the level of brokerage fees in relation to the rate of interest. Suppose that they decide to retire debt. In this case the excess supply of money by the active investors generates an excess demand for bonds by the passive investors and the rate of interest falls, a fall which is predicted by both theories of the rate of interest. But this means that the rate of interest reverts to the level at which it stood at the beginning of the period. Alternatively, suppose that stockholders decide to hold the additional cash voluntarily at an unchanged rate of interest. In that case the excess supply of money on the part of active investors generates an excess demand for money of equal magnitude on the part of passive investors. Consequently, the net excess demand for money (excess supply of bonds) which does actually appear on the market is zero. The rate of interest therefore stands at the new higher level at the end of the period. But this is consistent with both theories of the rate of interest.

Similar conclusions would follow if we assume that there is no Lundberg lag and that the increased demand for capital goods is met by an increase in current production either because no inventories are held, or because stockholders plan and succeed in making good by the end of the period the depletion of their inventories which occurred because of their sales to active investors. The resulting increase in the income of the producers of capital goods is assumed to result in no induced consumption or investment expenditure on their part within the current period. Therefore, like the passive investors in the Lundberg lag case, the only decision which they can take concerns the composition of their portfolios.

The foregoing can be illustrated within an amended form of the IS LM version of the income expenditure model. In Fig.1, the IS curve (the curve of equation (1)) is common to both models. Given the price level and the nominal stock of money, it depends on planned expenditure and the rate of interest. In the usual model (Model I), the curve of the monetary sector (the curve of equation (3a)) is $\overline{LM}$. It depends on actual output and the rate of interest. But in Model II, the curve LM (the curve of equation (3b) depends on planned expenditure and the rate of interest. Consequently, its slope is less steep referred to the Y axis than is that of LM. Both models have the same equilibrium solution provided that the amount of cash which is required to finance a unit of consumption is the same as that which is required to finance a unit of investment expenditure. This must be the case since equation (3b) is a linear combination of the same equations as are used to obtain the equilibrium values of the usual system. Hence, for purposes of comparative statics, there is no difference between the two models[16]. However, there is a difference in one-period dynamic analysis. For we have already seen that in the dynamic formulation of the usual model, with a one-period lag on the output variable in the equations of the expenditure and monetary sectors, the rate of interest cannot alter following a change in autonomous expenditure until income alters. Hence in that formulation, the IS LM framework is not appropriate unless actual and planned outlays on goods are equal, i.e. unless $S = I$. This difficulty does not arise when LM is the curve of the monetary sector. For example, when IS_0 shifts to IS_1 since LM_0

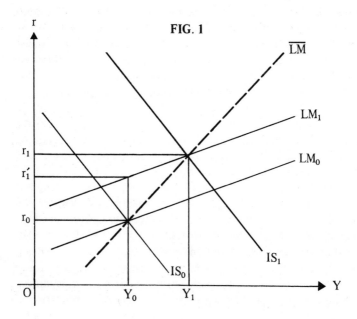

FIG. 1

contains the parameters of the expenditure functions, it shifts to LM_t. Consequently, the increase in the rate of interest from r_0 to r_1 can be broken up into two parts: an increase from r_0 to r_1', which is due to an increase in the transaction demand at the level of output Y_0 at which, given the autonomous increase in demand, saving is not equal to investment; an increase from r_1' to r_1 which is the result of the induced change in aggregate spending at the level of income Y_1 where $S = I$. In the model with inventories, the rate of interest will stand at this new higher level at the end of the period if passive investors do not retire the appropriate amount of debt. If they do retire debt, the rate of interest falls back to r_0 and then rises along $\overline{LM}$ to r_1 as income expands in the subsequent period. Thus the amended IS LM framework is a valid analytical apparatus which may be used to portray changes in the rate of interest which occur when output is constant, planned expenditure and actual outlays are unequal.

(ii) Consider next a shift in liquidity preference which is the result of a change in the uncertainty with which wealth-holders view the future. Such a change might make wealth-holders reduce their asset holdings of money and bonds and increase their demand for goods. When this is so, the analysis begins with all markets being simultaneously in disequilibrium. This is the case in which Patinkin (27) argues that the two theories are different and that the L.P. theory is a priori untenable inasmuch as it implies that the price of bonds can fall (rise) in the face of excess demand (excess supply) in the bond market. He puts the matter thus:

> "Under certain circumstances an excess supply of money may be accompanied by such a large excess demand for commodities that individuals will attempt to finance their additional purchases not only by using up all their excess cash, but also by selling part of their bond holdings."

The proposition is $X_g = -(X_m + X_b)$. Since the L.P. theory states that the rate of interest changes if and only if the excess demand for money is non-zero, Patinkin goes on to argue that this particular situation shows it to be implausible.

> "For it is difficult to understand why an excess supply of money should drive up the price of bonds even when there exists an excess supply of the latter."

Let us examine the matter more closely. Suppose that at the beginning of the period the excess demand for money being zero, equilibrium is disturbed by the desire on the part of some individuals to exchange goods for bonds. This is the case which we have already analysed and, as we have seen, in order to make these desires effective, there must first be a successful exchange of bonds for money followed by an exchange of money for goods. But the excess demand for money is not zero at the beginning of the period. For, concurrent with the excess demand for goods and the excess supply of bonds, there is an excess supply of money induced by an autonomous shift in the demand for money to hold as an asset which is not in favour of bonds but in favour of goods. This by itself would result in a reduction in the interest rate. But added to the excess demand for money which is generated by the attempt to substitute bonds for money, it simply ameliorates the rise in the interest rate. In other words, as a result of a simultaneous disequilibrium in all markets, we have as the first transaction, $-X_b = X_M - X_{\overline{m}}$, $(X_M - X_{\overline{m}}) > 0$ where X_M is the total sum of money which is required to finance the excess demand for goods and $X_{\overline{m}}$ is the part of the required finance which is to be supplied from the reduction in the stock of money which is held as an asset. Thus, in terms of the dichotomised budget constraint, we have an increase in the transactions demand for money in the income constraint, which is partly offset by the reduction in the asset demand in the expenditure constraint. Therefore the net excess demand for money, which is what actually appears on the market, is positive and equal to the value of the excess supply of bonds. But this results in a rise in the interest rate as predicted by the L.P. and the L.F. theories. (If we were considering a case where there was a shift against money as an asset and in favour of both goods and bonds, i.e. $X_g + X_b = -X_m$, there would be in the first instance a fall in the rate of interest as a result of the exchange of money for bonds, and this would be predicted by both theories.) Whether the rate of interest stands at this new higher level at the end of the period or reverts to the level at which it stood at the beginning of the period depends, as we have seen, on the asset behaviour of passive investors who face an unplanned reduction in their inventories.

However, an alternative interpretation of the sequence of events which is implied by the quotation from Patinkin is that individuals do not acquire all the cash they require before they begin to demand goods. In terms of our analytical framework we may assume that there is simultaneously an excess demand for goods equal in value to the excess supply of money from 'idle' balances and an excess transactions demand for money which is equal in value to the excess supply of bonds. Now, so far as the excess supply of bonds is concerned, this is matched by an excess demand for money, and this would result in a rise in the rate of interest as predicted by both theories. However, there is simultaneously an excess supply of money which is the result of the reduction in liquidity preference and which is spent directly on goods. As we have already seen, this taken by itself would generate an excess demand for bonds causing the rate of interest to rise, or an excess demand for money causing the rate of interest to remain unchanged according to whether stockholders do or do not retire debt in the face of an unplanned increase in their cash balances. Suppose that they retire debt. There would then appear simultaneously in the market an excess transactions demand for money (equal to the excess supply of bonds of the transactors who are attempting to obtain increased transactions balances) as well as an excess supply of money (excess demand for bonds) on the part of passive investors who have obtained excess money balances from the unplanned increase in their sales. Consequently, the observed change in the rate of interest will depend on their relative magnitudes falling, rising, or remaining unchanged according to whether the excess demand falls short of, exceeds, or equals the excess supply. In addition, the rate of interest will fall to the level at which it stood at the beginning of the period when transactors use the proceeds of the sale of bonds to purchase goods and stockholders use the excess cash to retire debt. If passive investors do not retire debt, the rate of interest rises as a result of the excess demand for transaction balances (excess supply of bonds) and is not affected by the purchase of goods, which is financed by the reduction in liquidity preference or by the proceeds of the sale of bonds, since this excess supply of money is matched by the excess demand of passive investors.

Thus whatever sequence of events we postulate, the behaviour of the rate of interest is the same whether we use the L.F. or the L.P. theory. It therefore appears that Patinkin's argument is incorrect because it relies on Walras' Law and on a form of the budget constraint which is inappropriate to the analysis of disequilibrium situations in a money economy.

It is also possible to show that both theories imply the same behaviour of the interest rate in response to changes in other parameters of shift.

Since we have seen that the Liquidity Preference theory, rationalised in terms of inelastic price expectations on the part of all wealth holders, plays a crucial role in the short run theory of the determination of the level of employment, it is reassuring to know that we need not abandon it when, within the framework of the income expenditure model, we wish to analyse changes in the rate of interest which occur when the market for goods is not in equilibrium.

NOTES

12 A detailed analysis of this question is given in (14).
13 This raises the well-known difficulty that, since the capital stock is assumed to be fixed, the period must be so short that changes in the capital stock will only have a second order effect on aggregate supply, but that it must also be long enough for the multiplier to work itself out.
14 Our proposition is that the transactions demand for money should be written as:

$$M_T = \alpha C + \beta I = \alpha Y + (\beta - \alpha)I \qquad (1)$$

$$\beta \neq \alpha \text{ or } \alpha = \beta, \ 0 < \alpha < 1, 0 < \beta < 1$$

instead of as:

$$M_T = kY, \ k = \alpha \ \text{ or } \ \beta < k < \alpha \qquad (2)$$

Using the notation of note 16 so that $\alpha = L_Y$ and $\beta - \alpha = L_I$, when M_T is written as in (1), LM is given by:

$$r = \frac{M^O - L_Y a_1 - (L_I + L_Y)a_2}{D} - \frac{L_Y C_Y - (L_I + L_Y)F_Y}{D} Y \qquad (3)$$

$$D = L_Y C_r + (L_I + L_Y)F_r + L_r$$

When M_T is written as in (2), $\overline{LM}$ is given by:

$$r = \frac{M^O}{L_r} - \frac{L_Y}{L_r} Y \qquad (4)$$

The curve of equation (3) clearly shifts with shifts in the expenditure function, whereas the curve of equation (4) does not.

15 Since plans to buy and plans to sell as well as their execution are conceptually and sequentially distinct operations in a money economy, it has been suggested (6) that the budget constraint of traditional theory is not an appropriate representation of the constraints which do face transactors in a money economy. A clear distinction between constraints on sales and constraints on purchases requires that we replace the traditional budget constraint

$$\sum_{i=1}^{n-1} p_i q_{ij} - M_j - M_j^o = 0$$

where M_j and M_j^o are desired and initial money balances respectively by an income constraint

$$\sum_{i=1}^{n-1} p_i q_{ij} - m_{jt}^t = 0, \quad q_{ij} \equiv d_{ij} - s_{ij}, \qquad q_{ij} \leqslant 0$$

and an expenditure constraint

$$\sum_{i=1}^{n-1} p_i q_{ij} - M_j^{ot} + M_j^t = 0, \qquad q_{ij} \geqslant 0$$

where m_j^t = receipts in period t

M_j^t = desired money balances held at the end of period t

and $M_j^{ot} = m_j^t + M_j^{t-1}$ = initial money balances held at the beginning of period t.

"The expenditure constraint asserts that all (net) purchase offers must be backed by a readiness to supply money in exchange. Thus M_j^t corresponds to the excess demand for precautionary money balances, i.e. total initial cash balances less prospective (gross) depletions of cash balances for currently scheduled purchases of goods. It follows that the total value of goods demanded cannot in any circumstances exceed the amount of money held by the transactors at the outset of the period. The income constraint asserts that all (net) offers involve a demand for just one other commodity, namely money in exchange. Thus m_j^t corresponds to what is commonly referred to as a demand for transaction balances (to replace cash) currently scheduled for disbursement from initial holdings of money balances." (6) It then follows that what is analogous to Walras' Law in a money economy is the proposition that "the money value of the sum of all excess demands, including the excess demand for reservation balances and for money income is identically zero" (6). In a full equilibrium when all excess demands are zero this is obviously equivalent to the usual statement of Walras' Law. (We have reformulated Clower's formal statement of the dichotomised budget restraint to avoid the possibility that the conventional budget constraint can be derived as a linear combination of the income and expenditure constraints.)

16 To analyse the consequences for the equilibrium level of income and the rate of interest of the alternative assumptions concerning the transactions demand, let us rewrite the relevant equations in the text as follows, noting that in equilibrium $Y_t = Y_{t-i}$ all i .

$$C\,(r, Y) - Y + I = -a_1 \tag{1}$$

$$F\,(r, Y) - I \quad\;\; = -a_2 \tag{2}$$

$$L_O\,(r, Y) \qquad = M^O \tag{3}$$

$$L_1\,(r, Y, I) \qquad = M^O \tag{3a}$$

Assuming a given price level, in Model II the equilibrium solution of income and the rate of interest is:

$$\overline{Y}_{II} = \left[L_r(a_1 + a_2) + F_r(a_1 L_I + M^O) + C_r(M^O - a_2 L_I) \right] / A$$

$$\overline{r}_{II} = \left[M^O(1 - C_Y - F_Y) - L_Y(a_1 + a_2) \right.$$
$$\left. - L_I \left\{ a_1 F_Y + a_2(1 - C_Y) \right\} \right] / A$$

where $A = \begin{vmatrix} C_r & C_Y - 1 & 1 \\ F_r & F_Y & -1 \\ L_r & L_Y & L_{I'} \end{vmatrix} = \begin{array}{l} L_r(1 - C_Y - F_Y) + L_Y(C_r + F_r) \\ + L_I \left\{ C_r F_Y + (1 - C_Y)F_r \right\} \end{array}$

In Model I, the solution is:

$$\overline{Y}_I = \left[L_r(a_1 + a_2) + (F_r + C_r) M^O \right] / B$$

$$\overline{r}_I = \left[M^O(1 - C_Y - F_Y) - L_Y(a_1 + a_2) \right] / B$$

where $B = \begin{vmatrix} C_r & C_Y - 1 & 1 \\ F_r & F_Y & -1 \\ L_r & L_Y & 0 \end{vmatrix} = L_r(1 - C_Y - F_Y) + L_Y(C_r + F_r)$

a_1 and a_2 are parameters of shift of the consumption and investment functions respectively, C_r is the marginal propensity to consume with respect to the rate of interest, C_Y is the marginal propensity to consume with respect to income, F_r is the marginal propensity to invest with respect to the rate of interest,

F_Y is the marginal propensity to invest with respect to the level of income, L_r is the proportion of resources which is held in the form of money for speculative purposes, and $L_Y = \alpha$ and $L_I = \beta - \alpha$ where α and β are the proportions of resources which are held in the form of money to finance a unit of consumption expenditure and investment expenditure respectively. We assume $C_r < 0, 0 < C_Y < 1$, $F_r < 0, F_Y > 0, L_r < 0, L_Y > 0, L_I > 0$. In equations (3) and (3a) it is assumed that L_Y is the same and is equal to α. It is also assumed that in (3a) $L_I = \beta - \alpha$. However, it is readily established that the qualitative results which we shall presently obtain are not affected if in Model I we postulated $M_T = kY$ instead of $M_T = \alpha Y$, $\beta < k < \alpha$.

As pointed out in the text, both models have the same solution so long as the amount of cash which is required to finance a unit of consumption is the same as that which is required to finance a unit of investment expenditure, i.e. so long as $\alpha \equiv \beta$. When they are not the same, the models have different equilibrium solutions; the values of the parameters determine which has the higher Y and the lower r. The models also yield different results in comparative statics. This is readily established by differentiating the equilibrium conditions of both models with respect to the parameters of shift, a_1 and a_2, and the stock of money.

	Model I	Model II
$\dfrac{dY}{da_1}$	L_r/B	$(L_r + F_r L_I) / A$
$\dfrac{dr}{da_1}$	$-L_Y/B$	$-(L_Y + L_I F_Y) / A$
$\dfrac{dY}{da_2}$	L_T/B	$(L_r - C_r L_I) / A$
$\dfrac{dr}{da_2}$	$-L_Y/B$	$-\{L_Y + (1 - C_Y) L_I\} / A$
$\dfrac{dY}{dM^o}$	$(F_r + C_r)/B$	$(F_r + C_r) / A$
$\dfrac{dr}{dM^o}$	$(1 - C_Y - F_Y)/B$	$(1 - C_Y - F_Y) / A$

In the general case when actual income and equilibrium income are not necessarily the same so that $Y_t \neq Y_{t-i}$ all i, the general solutions for Y and r are:

$$Y_t = C^t (Y_0 - \overline{Y}) + \overline{Y}$$

$$r_t = C^t (r_0 - \overline{r}) + \overline{r}$$

where $\overline{Y}$ and $\overline{r}$ are the equilibrium solutions. The equilibrium is locally stable if $0 < I \ C \ I < 1$.

In Model II

$$C_{II} = \frac{L_I (C_Y F_r - F_Y C_r) + L_r(C_Y + F_Y)}{L_r + L_I F_r + L_Y(C_r + F_r)}$$

In Model I

$$C_I = \frac{L_r(C_Y + F_Y)}{L_r + L_Y(C_r + F_r)}$$

Clearly then the two models imply different time profiles for income and the rate of interest in a disequilibrium situation even in the case in which they both have the same equilibrium solution, i.e. when it is assumed that $\alpha \equiv \beta$.

V Beyond the Economics of Keynes

The question which we must now ask is where do we go from here? Leijonhufvud thinks that we should not at this late stage go over the theoretical questions raised in the Keynesian debate. Instead, we should carry on Keynes' work by exploring informational problems in cybernetic systems. Whatever the case for such a programme, there do seem to be important issues to be explored which will involve a return to some of the issues which were raised in the great debate.

For one thing, it is important to know whether setting up a formal model, which follows that of Keynes more closely than does the income expenditure model, will provide a better vehicle for the development and systematisation of what we now consider to be his important and relevant insights into the behaviour of disequilibrium processes. For another, we must continue to extend the work begun by Keynes of integrating wealth concepts into our income models. There would be a considerable pay-off from analysing income determination models with as rich a menu of assets as is contained in the 'Treatise' (18). As Leijonhufvud notes, for this to be a fruitful exercise, we may have to abandon the prevalent notion that net worth is the only appropriate concept of wealth, as well as the view that only the aggregate net worth of the private sector influences aggregate expenditure. We must construct models which systematically take into account the interior of the matrix of claims, the asymmetry in the position of debtors and creditors and the role of bankruptcies. In such a framework we might be able to make a proper assessment of the contribution of Gurley and Shaw (10). We might also find that there is no one to one correspondence between the inter-connected set of real variables and the corresponding financial structure — a question which worried the authors of the Radcliffe report.

Then there is the theoretical question of how, if at all, a general equilibrium model moves from a Keynesian under-employment state to a long run equilibrium. Many economists feel that, in a full equilibrium of the system, the Walrasian model in its static or steady state version is appropriate. In this model, the values of the real variables are governed by real forces. In such an equilibrium money is unimportant; it simply determines the absolute level of prices. Money as a commodity with properties which distinguishes it from other commodities probably plays no essential role in such a system. The phenomenon of liquidity preference is absent since, along a steady state path, all expectations are fulfilled. However, in the short run, most of us consider that some sort of Keynesian model is appropriate. The theoretical question is therefore this: given some disturbance which generates a Keynesian disequilibrium state, does the system, given time, necessarily converge to the Walrasian equilibrium or does it converge to some other equilibrium? No satisfactory answers to these questions exist. That this is the case might very well be due to the resurgence and dominance of the Neo-Classical paradigm buttressed by the Neo-Classical synthesis, which rests on the proposition that Keynesian policies are required to ensure full employment but that once full employment is attained, the Neo-Classical theory is valid. Arrow (1) has shown that this inference does not necessarily follow. Let us adapt his argument.

Let $W(g)$ be the Walrasian system and $K(g)$ be the system with built-in Keynesian instruments (g are parameters of fiscal and monetary policy). Full employment holds in $K(g)$ for only some values of the g parameters, whereas in $W(g)$ it holds for all values of g. If $g = g^*$ such that full employment is attained in $K(g^*)$, it is not obvious that theorems which are valid in $K(g^*)$ are also valid in $W(g^*)$. For example, fiscal and monetary policy cannot have the same effect in the two systems since full employment is invariably a property of the one but not of the other. Alternatively, the proposition might be that the quantitative or qualitative response of both systems to changes in parameters other than the parameters of fiscal and monetary policy is the same. However there is no a priori reason why this should be the case. For instance, the response of the two systems to a change in technology might be different if in $W(g)$ information about the appropriate market clearing inter-temporal price vector is known at zero cost to all transactors and there is complete price flexibility, whereas in $K(g)$ information concerning this vector is not available, so that the response of the system depends upon the uncertain and inelastic expectations which underlie the state of liquidity preference and the state of long run expectations. The inflexibility of reservation and actual prices which underlie these phenomena might very well be inescapably bound up with the properties of money and hence with the dominant characteristics of a money using economy.

These considerations induce considerable sympathy for the view (7) that current monetary growth models, which consist of a standard growth model into which one additional commodity called money is inserted but in which the existence of money is not rationalised and in which the money commodity plays no distinctive role, should be regarded as trivial extensions of existing real models which are themselves the steady state analogues of static general equilibrium models. Adding transactions and carrying costs to the standard model may, if done successfully, constitute a step forward. However, as Shubik (32) has noted, it is not unreasonable to suspect that given this conceptualisation, money will be a little mouse which will squeak at an asymptotically declining rate and will vanish in the full solution state of the model. Real money is a social institution. A model which is to include it in a meaningful way may have to specify explicitly the institutional set-up, including the laws concerning monetary contracts and bankruptcy, the role of financial intermediaries, etc. We must face up to the possibility that the theory of money and the theory of a monetary economy may necessarily have to be anchored into models of economies which are on-going concerns[17].

Finally, there is the question of the determination of the money wage rate.

In the unit period of the formal model of the General Theory the money wage rate is given (or has a time rate of change which is for all practical purposes not significantly different from zero). To study the behaviour of the model over time, we therefore need a theory of the money wage rate.

The Phillips curve appears to be a candidate for the post. It is not unreasonable to infer from his work on stabilisation policy in a growing economy that Phillips did conceive of his curve as fulfilling this role. However, the rationalisation of that construct in his classic article (30) is in terms of the supply and demand curves for labour of Neo-Classical theory. In this theory the demand for and the supply of labour are functions of the real wage rate and the demand curve for labour is the marginal product curve. But this already implies that there is a full employment level of aggregate demand and output. For it is only in such a situation that the marginal product curve can be taken to be the demand curve for labour in the sense that an increase in the demand for labour is <u>necessarily</u> associated with a reduction in the real wage rates. In such a framework, changes in money wage rates either reflect the adjustment of factor proportions to that which is optimal as of a predetermined level of output, or are associated with the existence and the resolution of conflicting ex ante excess demands which are assumed to be the result of differential foresight as between employers and employees such that they evaluate a given change in money wages at different expected price levels[18]. Indeed, in the hands of the Neo-Classical purists as evidenced in a recent volume of essays edited by· Phelps (29), the theory of the Phillips curve becomes a theory of <u>frictional</u> unemployment at <u>full</u> employment. The coup de grace is administered when the adaptive expectations hypothesis is invoked. For if price changes are fully and correctly anticipated, the Phillips curve becomes a vertical line in the $\dot{W}$, U plane. Many economists are uneasy about this conclusion. Some nevertheless feel that the theoretical analysis is unassailable. It is not unassailable. The theory of search unemployment which underlies this work is consistent with the Keynesian hypothesis of inelastic expectations and less than infinite price velocity in the unit period, and must be an integral part of a theory of the money wage rates. The missing link is an analysis of the system-wide implication of all this in a complex system of inter-dependent markets where there exists no guarantee that full employment will be maintained. In such a situation it is more fruitful to think of the aggregate demand for labour as being derived directly from the aggregate demand for goods, rather than from the substitutability between the services of labour and the services of other inputs at a given level of final demand. As aggregate demand varies, the relationship between employment and the real wage rate will depend on technology, market structures and the employment policies of firms. Thus, given the dominance in the economy of technologies which exhibit constant or falling cost with output, and/or given the prevalence of oligopolistic structures in the key sectors of the economy together with the overhead characteristics of much labour (implying a lagged response of employment to changes in output), output per man and the real wage rate actually increase with a rise in output and employment. Moreover, if we are to offer an analysis which is consistent with the inflationary processes which are actually observed in actual economies, we must abandon the framework of the perfectly competitive labour market together with the assumption of an invariable full-employment level of output.

We should therefore start the other way round and regard the money wage rate as the independent variable in the observed relationship between the rate of change of money wage rates and the level of unemployment. The Keynesian system viewed as a model in which the level of demand, and hence the level of unemployment, depends on the level of the money wage rate as of a given labour force and stock of money is an appropriate framework for the analysis. At any moment of time, it is assumed that there exists some positive unemployment which consists of demand deficient as well as of structural components, and which can be reduced by an increase in effective demand. The money wage rate is assumed to be determined in a manner which is substantially independent of the level, of aggregate demand. It is regarded as the outcome of bargaining in labour markets in which the situation corresponds most nearly to bilateral monopoly and in which the determination of the money wage rate requires explicit recognition of bargaining strategy and market power even though the bounds to a settlement may be set by 'economic' forces. The problem then is to find some way of representing in an operational form those forces which exert pressure upon the money wage rate independently of the level of demand for labour. It was hypothesised by Hines (13) that autonomous pressure to maintain or to increase money wage rates is related to union militancy and that the rate of change of unionisation should be taken as a proxy for militancy which is not a directly observable variable. For just as workers do not regard the value of their human wealth as perfectly variable in the unemployment state and hence resist cuts in their money wages, in a growing economy (which may or may not be in a state of full employment) workers, as well as other agents, expect that the value of their wealth, and hence their real income, should rise as national income rises. If Walras' auctioneer or his equivalent were available not only to ensure that all transactors were made aware of the feasible increases in real incomes, but also that these increases were distributed in a manner which would be acceptable to each transactor and which would also yield a level of aggregate demand consistent with actual transformation possibilities, all would be well. But there is no auctioneer. Moreover, in this situation individuals cannot rely on a fall in the aggregate price level to bring about the requisite increase in their real income. The transactor has no direct control over the price level. He does however have some control over the price of the services of the productive resource which he owns. It is therefore quite rational that workers, for example, should take steps (e.g. by combining in trade unions) to raise their money rates of remuneration[19]. And since there is no guarantee that the sum of the claims which are successful and the resulting level of aggregate expenditure will mesh with productive potential, the situation is clearly inflationary.

Suppose that in this setting owners of productive services put upward pressure upon their prices in an attempt to raise their real incomes. Specifically, suppose that there is an autonomous push on money wage rates. If the necessary finance is forthcoming, the increase in aggregate demand will generate an increase in output and a reduction in unemployment. However, given the existing level of excess capacity, the interdependence of changes in factor and product prices as well as the trend rate of growth of productivity, the resulting increase in real incomes may fall short of the expected increase. (In addition income may be redistributed between transactors according to their market and bargaining power and according to the relative fixity of those contracts which are made in money terms.) If this is voluntarily accepted by all agents, the process comes to an end. If it is not accepted, and the push on prices of factors and products is maintained or accelerated, and there are no monetary and/or fiscal restraints, money incomes, wages and prices continue to rise at an accelerating rate, while real output and real wages increase and unemployment falls at a decreasing rate. Thus asymptotically, unemployment approaches zero or some positive constant, the rate of change of prices and money wages approaches infinity and real wage and real output tend to levels which are determined by the real forces of productivity, thrift and technical progress. Such a sequence of events would clearly generate a Phillips curve-like relationship between the rate of change of money wage rates and the level of unemployment. Moreover, such a curve would not have the expected rate of change of prices as a parameter of shift. In this framework, the expected rate of price change is a factor which determines the force of the exogenous push on money wage rates.

This does not mean that money wages might not vary in response to a change in the level of unemployment resulting from changes in demand brought about by changes in aggregate expenditure. Nor do we wish to deny the possibility that the rate of change of money wage rates might be modified by an increase in unemployment which is the result of countervailing monetary and fiscal policy. However, it is possible that a policy of increasing the level of unemployment, which is intended to slow down the rate of inflation, may have no ameliorative effect on the rate at which money wages and prices are pushed up. Such a policy might even accelerate the rate at which wages and prices are pushed up, inasmuch as an increase in unemployment tends to reduce the rate of growth of real wages below their expected levels. Hence, it is quite possible that we may observe, as we do in fact observe, a strong positive relationship between the rate of change of money wage rates and some index of autonomous pressure on wage rates (say an index of union militancy) associated with a positive or a negative relationship between the level of unemployment and the rate of change of money wage rates depending on whether monetary and fiscal policy are passive in the face of autonomous increases in wages and prices, or whether a countervailing policy is successful or unsuccessful in slowing down the rate of change of money wages and prices.

*   *   *

*   *   *

The frontiers of economic theory are now really very exciting. The work of Keynes, which has now been re-interpreted in a theoretically relevant fashion, opens the way to a serious analysis of disequilibrium phenomena whether of the deflationary or inflationary variety. The re-switching debate and the Sraffa revolution hold out the possibility that questions of relative prices can be divorced from questions of distribution. If relative prices are determined independently of distribution, and if the latter depends on social and institutional forces, then the question of the ethics of alternative relative shares is again on the agenda. Building on the work of Edgeworth and Arrow, one detects the beginning of a new and more fruitful welfare economics.

The role of a paradigm as the prerequisite for 'normal' science has been well analysed by Kuhn (21). And yet one wonders whether the anomalies which arise in the Neo-Classical paradigm are not now sufficiently numerous and substantial as to call into question its usefulness as a framework within which every economic problem is to be analysed. No less an authority than Samuelson has observed: "it is possible to argue that . . . Western economists, far from being too divided among a number of competing schools, today present a united front that reflects too little basic disagreement on fundamentals". One now feels that we are probably at the beginning of what Kuhn calls a period of revolutionary science. This revolution will be conducted within a framework of rules and with the technical tools which are appropriate to a serious science. One's faith for the future is in a synthesis which will include the best of Ricardo, Marx, Keynes and the Neo-Classics. That synthesis, if it comes, will re-establish the claim of economics to be the fundamental theory of society.

*   *   *

NOTES

17 Work which is concerned with or related to these and similar matters is beginning to appear in the literature.

Many of the papers in (29) explore the problems of dynamic adjustment in labour and product markets at the micro level. They rely in part upon mechanisms such as the adaptive expectations hypothesis and the partial adjustment model, and attempt to derive optimal adjustment paths as the solution to a constrained optimisation problem, which has as arguments variables such as adjustment costs — costs of being out of equilibrium and rising marginal costs of rapid change. These models need improvement inasmuch as the adaptive expectations hypothesis does not allow for learning on the part of transactors over time. Moreover, in the case of the labour market, the theory of search unemployment, which underlies many of these papers, must be an integral part of any satisfactory theory of disequilibrium dynamics. However, as we have already pointed out, the missing link is an analysis of the implications of such behaviour for the level of aggregate employment and output.

Work is beginning to appear which owes its stimulus to Clower's seminal paper (5). P. Flavert ("Disequilibrium in a Macro-Economic Model" Papers in Quantitative Economics Quirk and Zarley (eds.) Univ. of Kansas Press 1968 and "On the Stability of Full Employment Equilibrium" Review of Economic Studies Vol. XXXVII, April 1970, pp.239—252) has considered the question of the global stability of macro models in which the dual decision hypothesis is applicable to the behaviour of transactors. H. Grossman ("Theories of Markets Without Recontracting" Journal of Economic Theory Dec. 1969, pp.477—479 and "A General Disequilibrium Model of Income and Employment" American Economic Review, March 1971) has analysed models of price-quantity behaviour in systems in which trade takes place at non-equilibrium prices. However, these authors only explore the system-wide implications of inappropriate vectors of current relative prices. They do not analyse systems which are in disequilibrium over time because of incorrect vectors of inter-temporal prices. It is this latter source of disequilibrium with which Keynes was primarily concerned. J. Williamson ("A Simple Neo-Keynesian Growth Model" Review of Economic Studies Vol. XXXVII, April 1970, pp.157—172) has presented a 'Keynesian' growth model which allows for fluctuations and which generates an income constrained short run equilibrium. However, as the author himself notes, his model takes both the state of long run expectation (the marginal efficiency of capital schedule) and the state of liquidity preference to be exogenous rather than endogenous in the long run.

Finally questions such as the structure of transactions in a monetary economy, the demand for money with non-trivial monetary properties, and equilibrium with transactions costs are beginning to be explored in studies such as F.H. Hahn "Equilibrium with Transactions Costs" Walras Lecture, New York 1969; R.M. Starr "The Structure of Exchange in Barter and Monetary Economies" and "Equilibrium and Demand for Media of Exchange in a Pure Economy with Transactions Costs <u>Cowles Foundation Discussion Papers</u> Nos.295 and 300; and J. Niehans "Money in a Static Theory of Optimal Payment Arrangements" <u>Journal of Money, Credit and Banking</u> Nov. 1969, pp.706–725.

18 The formal theory of the conventional version of the Phillips curve may be set out as follows:

$$N^d - N^s = f(\frac{W}{P} \bigg| Y) - g(\frac{W}{P} \bigg| Z) = 0 \qquad (1)$$

The Neo-Classical dynamic adjustment mechanism is:

$$(\frac{\dot{W}}{P})/\frac{W}{P} = \lambda \ [(N^d - N^s)/N^s] = \lambda \ (X) \qquad (2)$$

$$(\frac{\dot{W}}{P})/\frac{W}{P} = \dot{W}/W - \beta \ \dot{P}/P, \qquad \beta = 1 \qquad (3)$$

Suppose, following Phillips, that there exists a stable non-linear transform from X to U

$$X = \theta \ (U) \qquad (4)$$

θ being such that as $X \to \infty$, $U \to 0$, as $X \to 0$, $U \to a$, $a > 0$ and as $X \to -\infty$, $U \to 100\%$.

Then $\dot{W}/W = \lambda \ \theta \ (U) + \beta \ \dot{P}/P$, $\qquad \beta = 1 \qquad (5)$

Now $\frac{\partial \dot{W}/W}{\partial U} < 0$ and $\frac{\partial^2 \dot{W}/W}{\partial U^2} > 0$ so that, given $\dot{P}/P$, the Phillips curve is convex and downward sloping.

If wages and prices were always flexible so that full employment was always attained, then U would always equal (a) and the Phillips curve would <u>always</u> be a vertical line in the W/W U plane. If, however, all wages and prices are not perfectly flexible within the unit period, specifically if all participants do not instantaneously adjust their price expectations to the going rate of inflation and renegotiate their money contracts accordingly, there will be a <u>short run</u> negative relationship between W/W and U.

In Fig.2 equilibrium in the labour market occurs at a position of 'normal' unemployment in which the real wage rate is constant or growing at a rate determined by the rate of growth of output given the rate of growth of population and the rate of technical progress. The actual and the expected rates of inflation are assumed to be equal. Suppose that some exogenous disturbance increases the actual rate of inflation. Since this was not expected by workers, the rise in money wages which is offered by employers to attract labour in order to increase output, results in an apparent rise in real wages from W_0/P_0 to W_1/P_0 and the supply of labour is increased from N_0 to N_1. However, since during a period of expansion, factor prices usually lag behind product prices, employers are now assumed to evaluate the real wage rate at a lower level namely W_1/P_1. There is therefore an expansion of employment, output and the rate of growth. But soon workers will come to realise that their real wages have fallen and they will take steps, which are assumed to be successful, to restore the status quo ante. There is therefore a reduction in observed employment and output until the system settles down (with or without oscillation) to the original equilibrium position or steady state path with the actual and expected rates of inflation being equal at new higher levels. Thus the trade off between the rate of change of money wage rates and the level of unemployment is temporary. To maintain the level of employment at N_1 requires an accelerating rather than a constant rate of inflation.

FIG.2

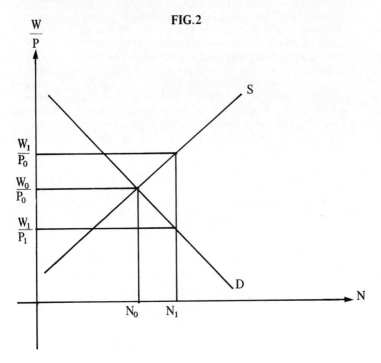

More formally, suppose that in equation (5) $\dot{P}/P$ is an inadequate proxy for the expected rate of change of prices $(\dot{P}/P)^*$, and that instead the formation of price expectations is governed by the adaptive expectations hypothesis, i.e.:

$$(\dot{P}/P)^*_t = k\,\dot{P}/P_{t-1} + (1-k)\,(\dot{P}/P)^*_{t-1} = \sum_{i=0}^{\infty} k(1-k)^i\,\dot{P}/P_{t-i-1}$$

Then $\dot{W}/W_t = \lambda\,\theta\,(U) + \alpha \sum_{i=0}^{\infty} k(1-k)^i\,\dot{P}/P_{t-i-1}$ (6)

In a full equilibrium, $\dot{P}/P_t = \dot{P}/P_{t-1}$ all t, $\dot{W}/W_t = \dot{P}/P_t$ all t and since $\sum_{i=0}^{\infty} k\,(1-k)^i = 1$, equation (5) can then be written as

$$\dot{W}/W = \frac{1}{1-\alpha}\,\lambda\,\theta\,(U) \qquad (7)$$

If $k = 0$ so that $\beta = 0$, we have a Phillips curve in which the trade off between unemployment and the rate of change of money wage rates is the same in the short run and in the long run. If $k = 1$ so that $\alpha = \beta = 1$ there is a trade off in the short run but not in the long run. If $0 < k < 1$ so that $0 < \beta < 1$, there is a trade off in both the long run and the short run though it is more favourable in the short run than in the long run. Solow (32a) and others have investigated this matter using U.K. and U.S. data and have invariably found $0 < k < 1$ so that $0 < \beta < 1$, which is contrary to the (Neo-Classical) generating hypothesis.

19 The question of why and under what conditions group and individual income is maintained or increased by combination, so that the optimising individual who has the option of bargaining on his own chooses voluntarily to belong to and bargain through a trade union in situations of rising aggregate demand (when, for example, the threat to quit is a potent bargaining counter for the individual) as well as in situations of falling aggregate demand, is a question which deserves to be examined.

Bibliography

1 K.J. Arrow "Samuelson Collected" Journal of Political Economy Vol.75, 1967, pp. 730–937
2 K.J. Arrow "Towards a Theory of Price Adjustment" in M. Abramovitz (ed.) The Allocation of Economic Resources Stanford Univ. Press, California, 1959
3 M. Bailey National Income and the Price Level: A Study in Macro Theory McGraw Hill, New York, 1962
4 W.J. Baumol "The Transactions Demand for Cash: An Inventory Theoretic Approach" Quarterly Journal of Economics Vol.66, Nov. 1952, pp. 545–546
4a A.B. Cramp "Does Money Matter?" Lloyds Bank Review, Oct. 1970, pp. 23–37
5 R. Clower "The Keynesian Counter-Revolution: A Theoretical Appraisal" in F. Brechling and F. Kahn (eds.) The Theory of Interest Rates proceedings of a Conference of the International Econ. Assoc. Macmillan, London, 1965
6 R. Clower "Reconsideration of the Micro Foundations of Monetary Theory" Western Economic Journal Vol.6 No.1, Dec. 1967, pp. 439–469
7 R. Clower "Comment: The Optimal Growth Rate of Money" Journal of Political Economy Vol.76, 1968, pp. 876–880
8 P. Davidson "Keynes' Finance Motive" Oxford Economic Papers Vol.17 No.1, March 1965, pp. 47–65
9 M. Friedman "The Quantity Theory of Money: A Restatement" in M. Friedman (ed.) Studies in the Quantity Theory of Money Chicago University Press, Chicago, 1956
10 J.G. Gurley and E.S. Shaw Money in a Theory of Finance Brookings Institution, Washington D.C., 1960
11 J.R. Hicks Value and Capital Oxford Univ. Press, London, 1939
11a J.R. Hicks "Mr. Keynes and The 'Classics': A Suggested Interpretation" Econometrica Vol.5, 1937, pp. 147–159
12 A.G. Hines and G. Catephores "Investment in U.K. Manufacturing Industry, 1956-67" in K. Hilton and D.F. Heathfield (eds.) Econometric Study of the United Kingdom Macmillan, London, 1970, pp. 203–224
13 A.G. Hines "Trade Unions and Wage Inflation in the United Kingdom, 1893–1961" Review of Economic Studies October 1964, pp. 221–252
14 A.G. Hines "Alternative Theories of the Rate of Interest: An essay in Monetary Dynamics" (mimeograph)
15 G. Horwich Money, Capital and Prices Richard D. Irwin, Homewood Illinois, 1964
16 H.G. Johnson "Keynes and the Keynesians: Some Intellectual Legends" Encounter Vol.34 No.1, Jan. 1970, pp. 70–73

17 N. Kaldor "The New Monetarism" Lloyds Bank Review No.97, July 1970, pp. 1–18

18 J.M. Keynes A Treatise on Money Macmillan, New York and London, 1930

19 J.M. Keynes The General Theory of Employment, Interest and Money Harcourt Brace, New York and Macmillan, London, 1936

20 J.M. Keynes "The General Theory of Employment" Quarterly Journal of Economics Vol.51, 1937, pp. 209–223

21 A.S. Kuhn The Structure of Scientific Revolutions Univ. of Chicago Press, Chicago, 1963

22 A. Leijonhufvud On Keynesian Economics and the Economics of Keynes Oxford Univ. Press, London, 1968

22a A. Leijonhufvud "Keynes and the Classics" Occasional Paper 30 Institute of Economic Affairs, 1969

23 R.C.O. Matthews "Expenditure Plans and the Uncertainty Motive for Holding Money" Journal of Political Economy Vol.71, 1963, pp. 201–218

24 F. Modigliani "Liquidity Preference and the Theory of Interest and Money" Econometrica Vol.44, 1944, pp. 45–88

25 F. Modigliani "The Monetary Mechanism and its Interaction with Real Phenomena" Review of Economics and Statistics (Supplement) Vol.45, Feb. 1963, pp. 79–107

26 R.A. Mundell "A Fallacy in the Interpretation of Macro-Economic Equilibrium" Journal of Political Economy Vol.LXXIII, 1965, pp. 61–66

27 D. Patinkin Money Interest and Prices Row, Peterson & Co., Evanston Illinois, 1956

28 D. Patinkin "The Chicago Tradition, the Quantity Theory and Friedman" Journal of Money, Credit and Banking Vol.1 No.1, Feb. 1969, pp. 46–70

29 E.S. Phelps et al. Microeconomic Foundations of Employment and Inflation Theory W.W. Norton, Co., New York, 1970

30 A.W. Phillips "The Relationship between Unemployment and the Rate of Change of Money Wage Rates in the United Kingdom 1862–1957" Economica Vol. XXV, 1958, pp. 283–299

30a The Committee on the Working of the Monetary System, Report, H.M.S.O., 1959

31 P.A. Samuelson "What Economists Know" in J.E. Stiglitz (ed.) The Collected Scientific Papers of Paul A. Samuelson M.I.T. Press, Cambridge Mass., 1966

32 M.J. Shubik "A Curmudgeon's Guide to Microeconomics" Journal of Economic Literature June 1970

32a R.M. Solow Price Expectations and the Behaviour of the Price Level Manchester Univ. Press, 1969

33 J. Tobin "The Interest Elasticity of Transactions Demand for Cash" Review of Economics and Statistics Vol.38, 1956, pp. 241–247

34 J. Tobin "Liquidity Preference as Behaviour Towards Risk" Review of Economic Studies Vol.25, Feb. 1958, pp. 65–86

35 W.E. Weber "Effect of Interest Rates on Aggregate Consumption" American Economic Review September 1970, pp. 591–600

36 L.B. Yeager "Methodenstreit over Demand Curves" Journal of Political Economy Vol.68, Feb. 1960, pp. 53–64

68